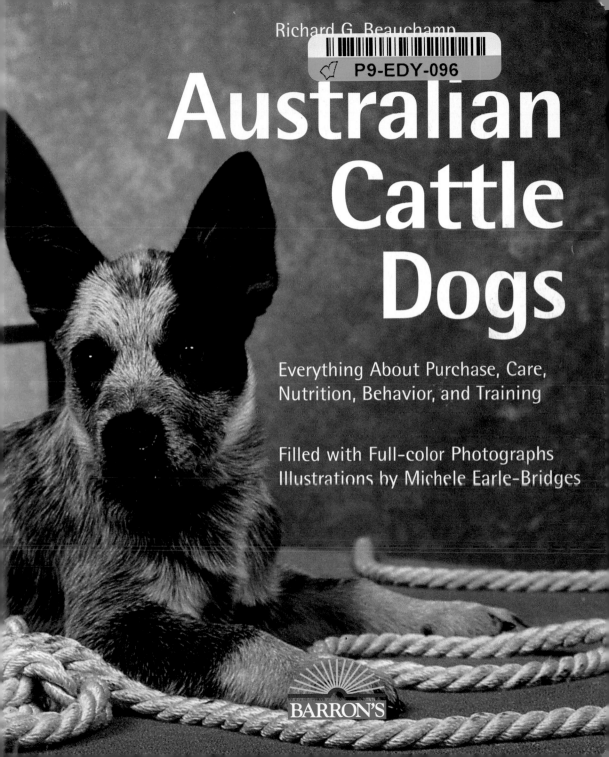

Richard G. Beauchamp

P9-EDY-096

Australian Cattle Dogs

Everything About Purchase, Care,
Nutrition, Behavior, and Training

Filled with Full-color Photographs
Illustrations by Michele Earle-Bridges

BARRON'S

CONTENTS

History and Origin of the Australian Cattle Dog 5

"Horses for Courses" 5

The Dingo 6

The First Australian Cattle Dogs 8

The Breed Today 11

The Australian Cattle Dog in the United States 13

Fanciers Unite 13

Versatility Events 14

Official Standard for the Australian Cattle Dog 14

Understanding Australian Cattle Dogs 19

Should You Own a Dog? 20

Why a Purebred Dog? 21

Is the Australian Cattle Dog the Right Dog for You? 23

Male or Female? 24

Where to Buy Your Australian Cattle Dog 24

Selecting an Australian Cattle Dog Puppy 27

What to Look For 27

Best Age for Selection 28

Show Dog or Companion? 29

Price 31

Veterinary Health Check 31

What You Must Get with Your New Puppy 31

Consider an Adult Dog 32

Importance of a Training Regimen 33

HOW-TO: Basic Puppy Training 34

Care of the Australian Cattle Dog Puppy 37

Preparing for the New Puppy 37

Bringing Your Puppy Home 39

"Puppy-Proofing" Your Home 39

Lifting and Carrying Your Puppy 40

The New Puppy and Other Pets 40

The Chase Instinct 41

Car Travel 41

Housebreaking 42

HOW-TO: Socialization and Safety 46

Care of the Adult Australian Cattle Dog 49

Prepare for an Active Dog 49

Outdoor Manners 49

Dealing with Behavior Problems 50

Spaying and Neutering 53

Toys 53

Instilling Good Behavior 54

Training Classes 54

Traveling with Your Dog 55

Your Aging Dog 56

The Last Good-bye 57

Feeding 59

Amount to Feed 59

Essential Nutrients 60

Canned Food or Dry? 60

The Appearance of Dog Food 61

Special Diets 61

Teaching Commands   63

The Sit Command   63

The Stay Command   64

Down   64

Heel   65

Bathing, Grooming, and Home Health Care   67

Equipment Needed   67

Brushing   68

Nail Trimming and Foot Care   68

Bathing   70

Home Health Care   71

Parasites   72

Vomiting and Diarrhea   75

Medical Problems   77

Immunizations   77

Emergencies   78

Illnesses   80

Inherited Health Problems and Diseases   82

Sharing Your Life with an Australian Cattle Dog   85

Enjoying the Breed's Versatility   85

Conformation Shows   86

How a Champion Is Made   87

Canine Good Citizen Test   88

Trials and Events   88

Fun and Games   90

Non-Competitive Pursuits   91

Information   92

Index   94

HISTORY AND ORIGIN OF THE AUSTRALIAN CATTLE DOG

When the early settlers began to migrate to Australia in the late 18th century, they realized many of the rules governing animal husbandry they had learned in their homeland had to be readjusted to this new and rugged environment. To help them deal with the challenges of their new homeland, the new Australians developed an incomparable herding dog. This was the Australian Cattle Dog.

"Horses for Courses"

"Horses for courses" is an old saying among British stockmen that has served as the basis for development of many kinds of prized livestock. Translated into layman's terms, this adage simply means choosing a formula that will produce a horse best suited to the terrain of the region in which the horse will work. This formula applied not only to horses but was the basis upon which many of Great Britain's outstanding livestock dogs were developed. This unique ability of the British was to be given its greatest test in the late eighteenth century.

The Australian Cattle Dog was created out of Australia's need for a rugged herding dog.

When the early settlers from the United Kingdom began to migrate to Australia in the 1780s they took their livestock with them. Once in the new country they realized many of the tried-and-true rules of animal husbandry they had brought from their homeland had to be readjusted to the rugged "land down under." The environment in which their livestock now lived differed dramatically and therefore the animals themselves behaved differently.

There were vast grazing lands available upon which the settlers could raise cattle and sheep. No longer confined by the space restrictions they had experienced in Great Britain, these immense land tracks encouraged stockmen to develop huge herds of not only sheep but also

There are two colors permitted in Australian Cattle Dogs—blue and red speckle.

husbandry might never have been able to meet. It was their long-practiced ability to develop "horses for courses" that saved the day and helped provide Australia with an economically successful cattle industry.

To help them deal with the myriad of problems their new homeland provided, the Australians developed an incomparable herding dog, a wonder dog so rugged, so uncannily intelligent, and so courageous that the breed was eventually to gain admiration and popularity throughout the entire world. This was the Australian Cattle Dog. The formula that produced this incomparable working dog is as fascinating as the breed itself. One must be familiar with the history of the Australian Cattle Dog in order to fully understand and appreciate the breed's unique nature and functional physique. The breed's story begins thousands of years before Western people had any knowledge that the island continent of Australia even existed.

of the more space-needy cattle. While an economic boon, the large herds were to create problems for ranchers they had not earlier been called upon to deal with. Because the cattle roamed the outback, unsupervised and unconfined, they were at best half wild. The cattle were not only difficult to keep track of but treacherous to the human hands hired to work with them.

British cattlemen had long relied upon the assistance of their highly developed sheepdogs to maintain the placid sheep and cattle in their homeland. However, these same dogs that had proven so capable in Great Britain met conditions in Australia they were ill equipped to cope with.

The new Australians were met with a challenge that a people less experienced in animal

The Dingo

Long before the first Europeans set foot on Australian shores there existed on that island continent a wolflike dog that the aboriginal population called *Worrigal* or dingo. It was first assumed the dingo had accompanied aboriginal people to Australia in their earliest migrations tens of thousands of years ago. Anthropological evidence has shown that aboriginal people have lived in Australia for at least 40,000–50,000 years; however, the irrefutable evidence of carbon dating actually places the oldest dingo fossil ever found at 3,450 years old. The mystery of how the dingo made its way to Australian shores has yet to be solved but there is no question that the dingo adapted to the rugged and varied Australian environment with great ease and enjoyed a pleasant coexistence with aboriginal man.

Research indicates the dingo is closely related to dogs that exist from Israel, east to Vietnam, north to the Himalayas, and southward through Indonesia, Borneo, and New Guinea. These all are descended from the Indian wolf rather than the northern timber wolf from which most other domestic dogs descend. It is theorized that semi-domesticated descendants of the Indian wolf accompanied the Indo-Malayan boat people in their migrations from Asia's mainland a little over 4,000 years ago and were used as barter and gifts.

The dogs that reached Australian shores evolved into what is known as the dingo, now afforded distinction as a separate subspecies of the domestic dog called *Canis familiaris dingo*. These dogs, which acclimated themselves to Australia, were never subjected to the same domestication pressures as the descendants of the northern timber wolf throughout Europe. Rather, they developed an independent yet close relationship with the aborigines. The dingo lived both in the aboriginal camps and in the wild. This simultaneous existence is documented by the writings of the earliest explorers who first tracked across the Australian continent.

The aborigines would take young dingoes from the nest, preferably before the pups' eyes were open, and would hand-feed or even suckle the youngsters. This human socialization process produced a relatively tame dog that was easily taught to track and hunt. The camp dogs were basically fed the same food their aboriginal owners ate. The dingoes that existed in the wild survived on a diet that consisted of the plentiful native game ranging in size from kangaroos to small rodents.

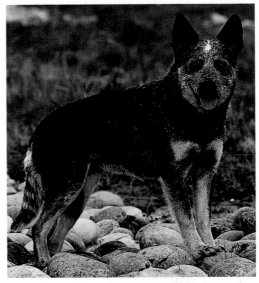

The history of the Australian Cattle Dog actually begins thousands of years before Western people arrived on the shores of the island continent.

Early written records describe dingo color as primarily shades of red. A few were black and tan or white. Pure dingoes were always seen to have a white tail tip and usually had white feet. The operative word here is "pure" in that dingoes readily mate with domestic dogs. Ticking or brindling of the white areas and piebald markings in the modern dingo are typical signs of cross-breeding with the domestic dog.

The Dingo as the Enemy of Humans

The dingo played an important role in the ecology of the land. It was a key figure in the checks and balances nature imposes and was respected for its role by the aborigines. The arrival of the vulnerable sheep herds in Australia provided a readily available diet alternative for the dingo.

Australian Cattle Dog breeders staunchly stand behind maintaining their breed's intelligence and working ability.

Its immediate addiction to sheep flesh quickly earned the dingo the reputation as a formidable enemy of pastoral people. The dingo was hunted and trapped without mercy but even at that it proved to be a wily adversary, surviving the harshest measures imposed for its eradication.

It is interesting to note that since the early European settlers despised the dingo for the havoc it wreaked upon their herds, they were grudgingly forced to respect the animal. No true stockman could do otherwise, for here was a canny survivor that could more often than not outmaneuver humans. These humans could not help but be aware and appreciative of the dingo's many survival attributes.

The dingo's determination and courage in the hunt knew no bounds. Dingoes do not bark, and they were able to swiftly and silently dispatch their prey. Their tireless conformation and incredible constitutions enabled them to cope with the most inhospitable temperatures and environmental conditions.

The stockmen's attempts to eradicate this livestock enemy only resulted in proving how uncannily intelligent these wild canines were. It was because of their awareness of the dingo's many adaptive characteristics that the new Australians turned to the native dog when it came time to employ the "horses for courses" formula they had relied upon in their original homeland.

The First Australian Cattle Dogs

The sensible, hard-working, and devoted dogs that were first used to work cattle in Australia found it difficult to handle the country's torrid summer temperatures, rough terrain, and vast distances that needed to be traversed. This was not the British Isles—not by a long shot! On top of that, the dogs barked incessantly, keeping the drovers' horses on edge and the near-wild cattle in a constant state of nervous frenzy that worried the hard-won fat right off their bones.

Several herdsman, seeing many of the qualities that their own dogs lacked in the dingo, attempted crossing their own herding breeds with the Australian native dog. These early crosses proved unsatisfactory because of their extreme aggressiveness. Left to their own devices the offspring of these matings would attack and eat sheep and could not control young calves.

It is extremely difficult to trace the exact history of the modern Australian Cattle Dog. The early pioneers of the breed often contradicted themselves in what breeds were crossed with the dingo to produce the dog they wanted.

My conversations with Cattle Dog breeders in Australia generally agree with what follows; however, this is not to say that different versions of the same story have not been written and passed on down by word of mouth.

It is said that in the year 1840, a certain Thomas Hall, who lived about 150 miles south of Sydney in the state of New South Wales, imported a pair of blue merle smooth-coated highland collies of a variety that no longer exists. He was disappointed to learn that, while they were willing and able sheepherders, neither the original pair nor their progeny were able to handle the fractious cattle or the hostile environment. Hall began experimenting with infusions of dingo blood and even the first crosses produced a dog that gave great promise.

The progeny of these original crosses worked silently. Instead of charging at the head of the

Stories handed down through generations indicate that many breeds of dogs were used to create the Australian Cattle Dog. Pictured behind the Australian Cattle Dog, left to right, are the smooth-coated collie, Dalmatian, kelpie, dingo, and the bull terrier.

cattle as their sheep-oriented collie ancestors did, the dogs worked from the rear, snapping at the heels of the cattle when needed. Working from the rear kept the cattle moving forward rather than challenging the dogs when they were charged from the head.

This first generation cross resembled small, heavily made dingoes. They were either blue-mottled or red-speckled in color. Reports of the successful cross spread throughout New South Wales and the neighboring state of Queensland. The breed grew in demand as word of their cattle herding ability grew. There was only one drawback to these smooth collie and dingo crosses—they tended to treat the stockmen's horses much like the cattle. They would often snap at the heels of the horses in a misguided attempt to have them join the cattle. Thus, it became obvious that any herding dog would have to have an amiable relationship with the drovers' horses.

A Dalmatian Cross

It is believed by most Australian Cattle Dog fanciers that Jack and Harry Bagust, who lived near Sydney, bred one of their best dingo and

Original Australian Cattle Dog Standard

Authored by Robert Kaleski, Sydney, Australia, 1902

Head (15 points):	Broad between ears, tapering to a point at muzzle, full under the eye, strong and muscular in the jaws.
Ears (10 points):	Short and pricked, running to a point at tip; thick and set wide apart on the skull with plenty of muscle at the butts. Should be as decidedly pricked as a cat's.
Eyes (7 points):	Brown, quick, and sly looking.
Shoulders (7 points):	Strong, with good slope for free action.
Chest (7 points):	Deep, but not out of proportion to body.
Legs (7 points):	Clean, fair amount of bone; very muscular.
Feet (7 points):	Small and cat shaped.
Back (7 points):	Straight, with ribs well sprung, ribbed up, and good loins; should arch slightly at loins.
Hindquarters (12 points):	Strong and muscular with back thighs well let down for speed; no dew claws on feet; tail, fair length "Dingo" or "bottle" shaped.
Height (7 points):	About 20 inches; bitches a little smaller.
Coat (7 points):	Short, smooth, and very dense.
Color (7 points):	Head, black or red; body, dark blue on back (sometimes with black saddle and black spot on tail butt). Lighter blue sometimes mottled with white hairs on underpart of body; legs, bluish, with red spots mottled over them. Tail light blue, sometimes with white tip.
TOTAL: 100 points	
General Appearance:	That of a small thickset blue Dingo.
Faults:	Over/or under size, legginess, half pricked or lopping ears, overshot or undershot jaws; anything likely to diminish speed and endurance.

smooth collie-cross females to a Dalmatian that had recently been imported from Great Britain. Their thought was to improve their Cattle Dog's rapport with horses, a characteristic for which the Dalmatian was long known. The offspring from this cross were born white as all Dalmatians are, but eventually developed blue speckle or red speckle coats at about three weeks.

The experiment was successful. The cross produced a dog that did in fact have a more workmanlike relationship with both horse and human. It is believed by some that a bull terrier cross was made at this time as well, but unfortunately, the herding ability and herding desire of the offspring were significantly diminished. As a remedy, breeders introduced the blood of the black and tan kelpie to the breeding program. The kelpies were a highly efficient Australian sheepdog. This produced a line of athletic dogs similar in type to the dingo but more muscular in build and distinctively colored.

The blue variety's body was dark blue, evenly speckled all over with a lighter blue. These dogs had black eye patches, black ears, and brown eyes. They also had tan legs, chests, and head markings. The red variety had dark red markings in place of black over an evenly speckled base.

Through selective breeding the dingo's athletic conformation and constitution, along with its intelligence and silent way of working, was maintained, as was the Dalmatian's devotion and protectiveness. This developing line of dogs was also heir to their sheepdog ancestor's ability to learn quickly and follow commands. The Australian stockmen had indeed developed "horses for courses." The wonder dogs were particularly useful in the huge, sparsely settled cattle stations in northern New South Wales and the neighboring state of Queensland. In fact, the breed became so popular in Queensland that the dogs eventually took on the name of Queensland Heelers or Queensland Blue Heelers.

In 1893 Robert Kaleski, a highly respected Australian journalist and noted dog fancier, became avidly interested in this new breed and became its first chronicler. It is through his efforts that type and color were fixed. From Kaleski's pen came the first written standard of excellence firmly based upon the breed's dingo heritage. In 1902 this standard was submitted to and adopted by the Cattle and Sheep Dog Club of Australia and the Kennel Club of New South Wales. The newly accepted breed was officially given the name Australian Cattle Dog though to this day many proud owners in Australia refer to their dogs as Queensland Heelers or Queensland Blue Heelers.

The Breed Today

The Australian Cattle Dog has changed very little in the past century. While conformation and color have become more consistent throughout, breeders have been staunch in insisting that the intelligence and working ability of this breed should not be diminished. To this day it retains its superior herding ability and has become a devoted and protective home companion as well.

Armed with a definitive standard it is only logical that Aussie breeders began to look to the show ring with their breed that had already gained the admiration of any self-respecting stockman in the country. Australian Cattle Dogs were shown along with other station stock at the local agricultural shows.

Usually, it was the rough-and-ready station owners who presented their dogs at the shows. Needless to say they and their dogs lacked the refinements developed in the less work-oriented breeds. While quality ran high, awards beyond the breed level were practically nonexistent; however, in the 1950s the breed made significant breakthroughs, particularly through the ring success of four dogs: Ch. Little Logic, his son Ch. Logic's Return, Ch. Trueblue Patches, and the all breed Best In Show winner, Ch. Hillside Duke.

THE AUSTRALIAN CATTLE DOG IN THE UNITED STATES

People in the United States were not unaware of the merits of the Australian Cattle Dog; American ranchers from coast to coast had imported working stock and found the breed effective on their side of the Pacific.

A turning point for the breed in America came in 1967 when Christina Risk and Esther Ekman met at a dog show and decided to form a club dedicated to the advancement of the Australian Cattle Dog as a dual purpose dog—working dog and show dog.

The name of the club they organized was The Queensland Heeler Club of America, a name popularly used throughout Australia and by many Americans who owned the working Cattle Dogs. On the advice of the American Kennel Club (AKC), however, the name of the club was changed to the Australian Cattle Dog Club of America and ground work for recognition of the breed by the AKC was outlined. Christina Risk was named president of the club that was then

The Australian Cattle Dog proved to be as valuable a working dog in America as it had been in its home country.

made up of Australian Cattle Dog owners who kept their dogs expressly as working stock dogs.

It was at that time that the newly organized fanciers discovered that, of the twelve-strong membership, only two of the members could actually trace their dogs' ancestry back to dogs registered in Australia. A painful decision was made by the founding members who agreed that the only dogs that would be accepted into the registry of the club were those whose ancestry could be validated with paperwork to the Australian registry.

Fanciers Unite

Popularity of the breed grew slowly and steadily and fans were attracted from among exhibitors of other breeds. The working Australian Cattle Dog entered an entirely new phase of its existence in America—that of a show dog—but existing club members united and vowed never to forget the breed's working ability and they began to develop ways to encourage this desire on the part of newcomers.

Versatility Events

This was accomplished in part by including versatility events at all the Fun Matches held from 1978 on. The matches were held to comply with AKC requirements for breeds seeking AKC approval. The Versatility Program was developed to encourage the breed's working instinct and obedience trainability. The club was adamant that the Australian Cattle Dog would not become a mere "dog show statue."

The winner of the first ACDA Fun Match was Tallawong Blue Joshua who was bred by Helen Dickson and listed in the show results as owned by "Spicer."

The Australian Cattle Dog has become a favorite at dog shows.

An official standard of the breed based upon the existing Australian standard was drafted and approved by the AKC in 1979. The Australian Cattle Dog was granted official AKC recognition on May 1, 1980 and the first AKC shows at which the breed could be exhibited were held on September 1, 1980. In 1984 the Australian Cattle Dog Club of America held its first AKC-sanctioned specialty show and obedience trial. There were 183 entries and the regular classes were judged by Janet Wilcox. The sweepstakes classes were judged by Jimmie Brookings and obedience by Barbara Goodman. The versatility class of 22 was judged by Dawn O'Reilly.

Ch. Billabong The Lodestone was the winner of the first National specialty. He was bred by Lois K. Moody and owned by Lois Moody and Jean Raviola.

Official Standard for the Australian Cattle Dog

General Appearance—The general appearance is that of a strong, compact, symmetrically built working dog, with the ability and willingness to carry out his allotted task, however arduous. Its combination of substance, power, balance, and hard muscular condition must convey the impression of great agility, strength, and endurance. Any tendency to grossness or weediness is a serious fault.

Characteristics—As the name implies, the dog's prime function, and one in which he has no peer, is the control and movement of cattle in both wide open and confined areas. Always alert, extremely intelligent, watchful, courageous, and trustworthy, with an implicit devotion to duty make it an ideal dog.

This picture portrays an Australian Cattle Dog of the type described in the AKC Breed Standard.

Temperament—The Cattle Dog's loyalty and protective instincts make it a self-appointed guardian to the Stockman, his herd and his property. Whilst naturally suspicious of strangers, must be amenable to handling, particularly in the Show ring. Any feature of temperament or structure foreign to a working dog must be regarded as a serious fault.

Head and Skull—The head is strong and must be in balance with other proportions of the dog and in keeping with its general conformation. The broad skull is slightly curved between the ears, flattening to a slight but definite stop. The cheeks muscular, neither coarse nor prominent with the underjaw strong, deep, and well developed. The foreface is broad and

well filled in under the eyes, tapering gradually to form a medium length, deep, powerful muzzle with the skull and muzzle on parallel planes. The lips are tight and clean. Nose black.

Eyes—The eyes should be of oval shape and medium size, neither prominent nor sunken and must express alertness and intelligence. A warning or suspicious glint is characteristic when approached by strangers. Eye color, dark brown.

Ears—The ears should be of moderate size, preferably small rather than large, broad at the base, muscular, pricked and moderately pointed, neither spoon nor bat eared. The ears are set wide apart on the skull, inclining outward, sensitive in their use and pricked when alert, the

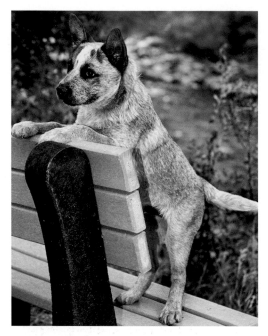

from the side. Although the shoulders are muscular and the bone is strong, loaded shoulders and heavy fronts will hamper correct movement and limit working ability.

Body—The length of the body from the point of the breast bone, in a straight line to the buttocks, is greater than the height at the withers, as 10 is to 9. The topline is level, back strong with ribs well sprung and carried well back not barrel ribbed. The chest is deep, muscular, and moderately broad with the loins broad, strong, and muscular and the flanks deep. The dog is strongly coupled.

Hindquarters—The hindquarters are broad, strong, and muscular. The croup is rather long and sloping, thighs long, broad and well developed, the stifles well turned and the hocks strong and well developed, the stifles well turned and the hocks strong and well let down. When viewed from behind, the hind legs from the hocks to the feet, are straight and placed parallel, neither close nor too wide apart.

Feet—The feet should be round and the toes short, strong, well arched and held close together. The pads are hard and deep, and the nails must be short and strong.

Tail—The set on of tail is moderately low, following the contours of the sloping croup and of length to reach approximately to the hock. At rest it should hang in a very slight curve. During movement or excitement the tail may be raised, but under no circumstances should any part of the tail be carried past a vertical line drawn through the root. The tail should carry a good brush.

leather should be thick in texture and the inside of the ear fairly well furnished with hair.

Mouth—The teeth, sound, strong, and evenly spaced, gripping with a scissor-bite, the lower incisors close behind and just touching the upper. As the dog is required to move difficult cattle by heeling or biting, teeth that are sound and strong are very important.

Neck—The neck is extremely strong, muscular, and of medium length broadening to blend into the body and free from throatiness.

Forequarters—The shoulders are strong, sloping, muscular, and well angulated to the upper arm and should not be too closely set at the point of the withers. The forelegs have strong, round bone, extending to the feet and should be straight and parallel when viewed from the front, but the pasterns should show flexibility with a slight angle to the forearm when viewed

The Australian Cattle Dog standard describes a dog whose construction allows for tireless all-day work with livestock.

Gait/Movement—The action is true, free, supple, and tireless and the movement of the shoulders and forelegs is in unison with the powerful thrust of the hindquarters. The capability of quick and sudden movement is essential. Soundness is of paramount importance and stiltiness, loaded or slack shoulders, straight shoulder placement, weakness at elbows, pasterns or feet, straight stifles, cow or bow hocks, must be regarded as serious faults. When trotting the feet tend to come closer together at ground level as speed increases, but when the dog comes to rest he should stand four square.

Coat—The coat is smooth, a double coat with a short dense undercoat. The outercoat is close, each hair straight, hard, and lying flat, so that it is rain-resisting. Under the body, to behind the legs, the coat is longer and forms near the thigh a mild form of breeching. On the head (including the inside of the ears), to the front of the legs and feet, the hair is short. Along the neck it is longer and thicker. A coat either too long or too short is a fault. As an average, the hairs on the body should be from approximately 1–1.5 inches (2.5–4 cms) in length.

Color (Blue)—The color should be blue, blue-mottled, or blue speckled with or without other markings. The permissible markings are black, blue, or tan on the head, evenly distributed for preference. The forelegs tan midway up the legs and extending up the front to breast and throat, with tan on jaws; the hindquarters tan on inside of hind legs and inside of thighs, showing down the front of the stifles and broadening out to the outside of the hind legs

from hock to toes. Tan undercoat is permissible on the body providing it does not show through the blue outer coat. Black markings on the body are not desirable.

Color (Red Speckle)—The color should be of good even red speckle all over, including the undercoat (neither white nor cream), with or without darker red markings on the head. Even head markings are desirable. Red markings on the body are permissible but not desirable.

Size—Height:

Dogs approximately 18–20 inches (46–51 cms) at withers

Bitches approximately 17–19 inches (43–48 cms) at withers

Faults—Any departure from the foregoing points should be considered a fault and the seriousness with which the fault should be regarded should be in exact proportion to its degree.

Approved: January 11, 1999
Effective: February 24, 1999

UNDERSTANDING AUSTRALIAN CATTLE DOGS

Given proper consideration beforehand, the purchase of an Australian Cattle Dog can bring many years of companionship and comfort as well as unconditional love and devotion. But it takes a great commitment on the part of the owner to help the breed reach its full potential.

People find Australian Cattle Dogs attractive for various reasons. Though the breed can hardly be described as "pretty," many find the breed's simple, natural lines very handsome. Others are attracted to the Australian Cattle Dog's legendary intelligence and ability to understand its owner. While these are but a few of the valid assets of the Australian Cattle Dog, they are still not enough reason for anyone to rush out to buy an Australian Cattle Dog.

This is not a breed that can be put outdoors in a pen and attended to only when the owner has the time or notion to do so. It is a breed that is capable of becoming a great companion and cherished friend, but only if the owner is ready to invest the necessary time and patience

Even though an Australian Cattle Dog may spend its life as a family companion, its herding heritage is never forgotten.

in the training that is required to help the breed achieve its full potential.

As one devoted Australian Cattle Dog owner put it, "Lots of people *think* they want an Australian Cattle Dog, but if they knew more about the needs of the breed, they wouldn't. Some breeds are said to constantly be one step ahead of their owners; Australian Cattle Dogs stay at least *three* steps ahead!"

All puppies are cuddly and cute and may even spend a part of their day duplicating all those popular and appealing greeting card and calendar poses; however, it is important to realize that a puppy will spend only a very small part of its day in such a docile state. The far greater part of the day and night the puppy will spend investigating, digging, chewing, eating, relieving itself, needing to go outdoors, and then immediately insisting that it be let in. All too often these needs are not

Puppies spend most of their day investigating, digging, chewing, eating, and relieving themselves. This all takes a great commitment on the part of the owner.

realistically considered before adding a dog to one's household.

The list of the real needs of a young puppy or an adult dog can be staggering to the uninitiated, and it takes a very concerned and dedicated owner to fulfill these needs, to say nothing of the time required for the many lessons an Australian Cattle Dog must be taught by its master before it understands what it may and may not do.

Friends often seek our advice when they are contemplating the purchase of their first dog. If we detect even the slightest uncertainty on their part, we always advise them to wait until they are absolutely sure they want to take on this great responsibility. Owning a dog, particu-

larly an Australian Cattle Dog, takes a great commitment and it is not something that should ever be done on a whim. The hasty purchase of a dog can result in sheer drudgery and frustration for the owner, and an unhappy situation for the dog itself.

Failure to understand the amount of time and consideration a well-cared for dog requires is one of the primary reasons for the number of unwanted canines that end their lives in an animal shelter. Given proper consideration beforehand, the purchase of a dog can bring many years of companionship and comfort as well as unconditional love and devotion no other animal can match.

Should You Own a Dog?

Consider three very important questions:

1. Does the person who will ultimately be responsible for the dog's day-to-day care really want a dog?

In many active families the woman of the household is the person who will have the ultimate responsibility for the family dog and she may not want any more duties than she already has. Pet care can be an excellent way to teach children responsibility, but beware—in their enthusiasm to have a puppy, children are apt to promise almost anything. It is what will happen after the novelty of owning a new dog has worn off that must be considered.

2. Does the lifestyle and schedule of the household lend itself to the demands of proper dog care?

This means there must always be someone available to see to the dog's basic needs: feeding, exercise, coat care, access to the outdoors when required, and so on.

3. Is the kind of dog being considered suitable for the individual or household?

Very young children can be very rough and unintentionally hurt a young puppy of a small breed. On the other hand, a young dog of a very large or very rambunctious breed like the Australian Cattle Dog can overwhelm and sometimes injure an infant or small child in an enthusiastic moment. Sharing a tiny apartment with a giant breed can prove extremely difficult for both dog and owner. Toy breeds will have difficulty surviving northern winters if required to live outdoors in unheated quarters. A long-haired dog, while attractive, is hardly suitable for the individual who spends most outdoor time camping, hunting, or hiking through the woods.

In addition to the above three major questions regarding dog ownership, the prospective dog owner should strongly consider the specific peculiarities of his or her own lifestyle or household. All this applies whether the household is made up of a single individual or a large family. Everyone involved must realize that the new dog will not understand the household routine and must be taught *everything* you want it to know and do. This takes time and patience, and very often the most important lessons for the new dog to learn will take the longest for it to absorb.

Why a Purebred Dog?

There is no difference in the love, devotion, and companionship that a mixed-breed dog and a purebred dog can give its owner. There are, however, some aspects of suitability that can best be fulfilled by the purebred dog.

All puppies, purebred or not, are cute but it stands to reason that not all puppies will grow up to be particularly attractive adults. It is nearly

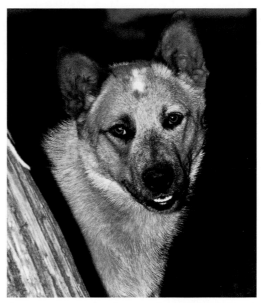

Given proper consideration beforehand, the purchase of an Australian Cattle Dog can bring many years of companionship and comfort to the entire family.

impossible to predict what a mixed-breed puppy will look like at maturity. Size, length of hair, and temperament can vary widely and may not be at all what the owner had hoped. Then what happens to the dog?

In buying a purebred puppy, the purchaser will have a very good idea of what the dog will look like and how it will behave as an adult; purebred dogs have been bred for generations to meet specifications of conformation and temperament.

When choosing a puppy, one must have the adult dog in mind because the adult dog should fit the owner's lifestyle and esthetic standards. A very fastidious housekeeper may have trouble accommodating a large breed that sheds its coat all year around. Joggers or long-distance runners

Although the potential buyer may find the sturdy good looks of the Australian Cattle Dog very attractive, the breed's temperament and need for exercise are an important consideration as well.

who want a dog to accompany them are not going be happy with a short-legged or slow breed. It is also important to know that short muzzled dogs and those with "pushed-in" faces have very little heat tolerance. Consider these points *before* you select a puppy.

Since the conformation of purebred dogs is entirely predictable, the owner of a purebred puppy will know that the breed he or she selects will still be appropriate as an adult. Temperament in purebred dogs has great predictability, although there may be minor variations within a breed. The hair-trigger response and hyperactivity of certain breeds would not be at all suitable for someone who wants a quiet, contented companion, nor would the placid attitude of other breeds be desirable for someone who wants an

athletic, exuberant dog to frolic with. With purebred dogs, you are reasonably assured of selecting a dog compatible with your lifestyle.

Price

The initial purchase price of a purebred dog will be a significant investment for the owner, but a purebred dog costs no more to maintain than a mixed breed. If the cost of having exactly the kind of dog you want and are proud to own is gauged over the number of years you will enjoy it, you will have to admit the initial cost becomes far less consequential.

Appearance

Before hastily buying a breed of dog whose *appearance* you find appealing, spend time with adult members of the breed or do some good research to assure yourself that you and the breed in question are temperamentally compatible. Many books have been written about the various breeds and often devote a good amount of space to discussing the temperament of the breed. Visiting kennels or breeders specializing in the breed of your choice will assist you enormously in deciding if you are considering the right breed for you.

Is the Australian Cattle Dog the Right Dog for You?

The Australian Cattle Dog was bred to work. At no time in its developmental history was any attempt made to make the breed a lapdog or boudoir companion. The Cattle Dog must be given something to do or it will think up something to do on its own—and that "something" just might be dismantling your new sofa or taking up your wall-to-wall carpeting. The Cattle Dog needs a lot of exercise. It is not an apartment dog that can be left alone in confined quarters day after day.

Deciding Who Is Boss

This is definitely a breed with a mind of its own. It will size up a situation and, if unaccustomed to looking to its owner for directions, will make decisions on its own and it will *act*. It has a hair-trigger response mechanism. Owners who have been negligent in making their Cattle Dog understand who makes all the rules will find themselves left out of decision making entirely. Remember the Cattle Dog's dingo heritage and its resultant need for a strong pack leader. If you do not provide that leadership, your dog will provide leadership for itself.

It takes a lot of dog to boss around a full-grown wild steer and what the Cattle Dog lacks in size, it easily makes up in aggression and tenacity. They were bred to *bite* the heels of cattle. The fact that there might not be any cattle heels around to bite does not diminish their desire to do so. If this is unharnessed, there could be a distinct problem.

With all that said, if a prospective owner is willing to take on the responsibilities required of a conscientious Cattle Dog owner, there are few breeds that can provide more devotion and companionship than this one. The Australian Cattle Dog lives to be with its owner and it can do that since it is a breed that is just about the right size to go anywhere—not too large and not too small, short of coat and long on endurance, tolerant of both heat and cold. Australian Cattle Dogs love the water and can swim great distances without

All puppies are cute, but that look is short-lived. The buyer must keep in mind what the adult dog will look like.

tiring. They love their home and do not have an urge to roam.

Male or Female?

While some individuals may have their personal preferences as to the sex of their dog, we can honestly say that both the male and the female Australian Cattle Dog make equally good companions and are equal in their trainability and affection. The decision will have more to do with the lifestyle and ultimate plans of the owner than differences between the sexes in the breed.

The male Cattle Dog is much taller and heavier boned than the female and does present one problem that the prospective buyer should consider. While both the male and the female must be trained not to urinate in the home, the male of any breed of dog has a natural instinct to lift his leg and urinate on objects to establish and "mark" his territory. The degree of effort that must be invested in training the male to not do this varies with the individual dog. This habit becomes increasingly more difficult to correct with the number of times a male dog is used for breeding, as the mating act increases his need and desire to mark his territory.

On the other hand, one must realize that the female is not problem-free. She will have her semiannual, and sometimes burdensome, heat cycle after she is eight or nine months old. At these times she must be confined in order to avoid soiling her surroundings, and she must also be closely watched to prevent male dogs from gaining access to her or she will become pregnant.

Altering

Both of these sexually associated problems can be eliminated by having the pet Australian Cattle Dog "altered" (see Spaying and Neutering, page 53). Spaying the female and neutering the male will not change the personality of your pet and will avoid many problems. Neutering the male Cattle Dog can reduce its aggressive attitude toward other males and will reduce, if not entirely eliminate, its desire to pursue a neighborhood female that shows signs of an impending romantic attitude.

It is important to understand though that these are not reversible procedures. If you are considering the possibility of showing your Australian Cattle Dog, altered animals are not allowed to compete in American Kennel Club or United Kennel Club conformation dog shows. They may, however, compete in herding and obedience trials, agility events and field trials.

Where to Buy Your Australian Cattle Dog

Your Australian Cattle Dog will live with you for many years. This is a breed that regularly enjoys a long, healthy life, living to be 12, 14, even 16 years of age. It is extremely important, therefore, that the dog comes from a source where physical and mental soundness are primary considerations in the breeding program, usually the result of careful breeding over a period of many years. Selective breeding is aimed at maintaining the virtues of the breed and eliminating genetic weaknesses. Because this selective breeding is time-consuming and costly, good breeders protect their investment by providing the best prenatal care for their breeding females and nutrition for the growing puppies. There is no substitute for the amount of dedication and care good breeders give their dogs.

The Australian Cattle Dog Club of America and the American Kennel Club (see Information, page 92) can provide the prospective buyer with the names and addresses of responsible individuals who have intelligently bred Australian Cattle Dogs that are available for sale. Many local pet stores will carry a list of good breeders and can refer you directly to them as well.

Breeders—What to Consider

There is a good chance that there are reputable breeders located nearby who will not only be able to provide the Australian Cattle Dog you are looking for but who will be able to advise you regularly in proper care and feeding. These breeders normally have the parents and other relatives of the dog you are interested in on the premises.

Health: Do not hesitate to ask questions and to ask to see the breeder's mature dogs. While there are relatively few hereditary defects that occur in Australian Cattle Dogs, experienced breeders know which hereditary problems exist in the breed and will be happy to discuss them with you. Practically all breeds are subject to inherited ailments and Australian Cattle Dogs are no exception.

Beware of breeders who tell you that their dogs are not susceptible to inherited diseases or potential problems. I do not mean to imply that all Australian Cattle Dogs are afflicted with genetic problems, but a reliable breeder will give you the information you are entitled to know regarding the individual dog you are considering. The subsection, Inherited Health Problems and Diseases, beginning on page 82, will give you details on some of the genetic ailments that might exist in this breed.

Temperament and health of the parents of your prospective purchase are of paramount

If the Australian Cattle Dog is not accustomed to looking to its owner for direction, it will make decisions on its own. This can cause trouble for both dog and owner.

importance. It is important that you see the parents, or at the very least, the mother, of your prospective purchase. If you dislike what you observe in either of them, *look elsewhere!*

Environment: Inspect the environment in which the dogs are raised. Cleanliness is as important to producing good stock as are good pedigrees. The time you spend in researching and inspecting the kennel and the adult dogs it houses may well save you a great deal of money and heartache in the years to come.

All this is not to imply your Australian Cattle Dog puppy must come from a large kennel. On the contrary, many good puppies are produced by small hobby breeders in their homes. These names may well be included in recommendations from both the American Kennel Club and the Australian Cattle Dog Club of America.

SELECTING AN AUSTRALIAN CATTLE DOG PUPPY

Living with an Australian Cattle Dog is a serious commitment. Whether you wish to have your dog as a companion or working partner, you will need to consider several things. With proper attention and care, the dog will be an active part of your life for many years.

What to Look For

The Australian Cattle Dog puppy you want to buy should be a happy, playful extrovert. Never select a puppy that appears frail or sickly because you feel sorry for it. Australian Cattle Dog puppies with positive temperaments are not afraid of strangers. Under normal circumstances you will have the whole litter in your lap if you kneel and call them to you. When the AKC breed standard states that the Australian Cattle Dog should be "suspicious of strangers," it is

Responsible breeders are always interested in making sure that every puppy they breed goes to the proper home.

referring to the adult dog. The adult Cattle Dog has developed territorial tendencies and the "suspicious" part of its nature is simply the dog's desire to protect home or owner from intrusion. A puppy will not have developed this part of its character and you definitely should avoid the puppy that cowers in a corner or one that tries to run away from you.

Ranchers in Australia have been known to pick their Cattle Dog puppy from a litter by calling to the puppies and walking away. The pup that reaches the caller first is the one that is chosen. If nothing else, this certainly makes a very strong comment on the fearless and friendly attitude of the well-bred Australian Cattle Dog puppy.

If one puppy in particular appeals to you, pick it up and, if possible, carry it off to an area nearby where the two of you can spend some time alone. As long as a puppy is still in a fairly familiar environment where scents and sounds are not entirely strange, it should remain relaxed and happy in your arms. Avoid the puppy that becomes tense and struggles to escape.

Physical Signs

When you and your prospective puppy are alone, you will have an opportunity to examine the puppy more closely:

✔ Check the puppy's ears. They should be pink and clean. Any odor or dark discharge could indicate ear mites, which in turn would indicate poor maintenance.

✔ The inside of the puppy's mouth and gums should be pink, and the teeth should be clean and white. There should be no malformation of the mouth or jaw.

✔ The dark eyes should be clear and bright. Again, be aware of any signs of discharge.

✔ Australian Cattle Dog puppies should feel compact and substantial to the touch, never bony and undernourished, nor should they be bloated; a taut and bloated abdomen is usually a sign of worms. A rounded puppy belly is normal.

✔ The nose of an Australian Cattle Dog puppy should not be crusted or running.

✔ A cough or diarrhea is a danger signal as are any eruptions on the skin.

✔ Conformation is important even at an early age. The puppy's legs should be straight. As the pup walks toward you, its front legs should move directly forward, as should the rear legs when the pup is moving away from you. The movement should be free and easy.

If you have been reading and doing your research, you can expect the Australian Cattle Dog puppy to look almost like a miniaturized version of an adult. The puppy coat is much softer than the adult coat but the hair should never be long or fluffy. Color and markings will be visible but much lighter than when the puppy matures. Cattle Dog puppies are born white and color develops as the puppy matures, darkening until it reaches adulthood.

Ears may already be standing but, if not, simply hold the puppy in your two hands and tilt its head downward. The ears will lie back and this will give you a picture of what the puppy will look like when the ears stand on their own. Ears may seem a bit large at this early stage, but more often than not the puppy will grow into them.

Helpful hint: Put the puppy on the floor and when it is busy investigating its surroundings, make a strange noise. The puppy should react and whirl around to see where the noise is coming from. If it does not react, you should definitely investigate the possibility of deafness. Deafness is a serious congenital defect in the breed. Responsible breeders test their breeding stock and the defect is far less a problem today than it was at one time. A responsible breeder will discuss the problem with you and insure you that the puppy you buy is sound in that respect.

Best Age for Selection

Raising a puppy is a wonderful experience. Granted, at times it can also be one of the most exasperating experiences you have ever attempted. In the end though, having endured each other through all the trials of puppyhood, you and your Australian Cattle Dog will forge a bond that has no equal.

A healthy puppy's eyes are clear and bright. Discharge of any kind could indicate a serious problem.

Should you decide that you do, in fact, wish to raise this little tyke from infancy to adulthood, be aware that most breeders do not and should not release their puppies until they have had their initial inoculations, which is at about eight to ten weeks of age. While they are nursing, puppies receive temporary immunity to diseases through their mother. Once they have been weaned, they lose this immunity and must be appropriately inoculated. Do not remove a puppy from its home environment before it has been vaccinated.

Prior to immunization, puppies are very susceptible to infectious diseases. Many such diseases may be transmitted via the clothing and hands of people. After the first series of vaccinations the breeder will inform you when your Australian Cattle Dog puppy is ready to leave its first home.

Show Dog or Companion?

If dog shows and breeding are in the future of your Australian Cattle Dog puppy, the older it is at the time of selection the more likely you will know how good a dog you will have at maturity. The most any breeder can say about an eight-week-old Cattle Dog puppy is that it has or does not have "show potential." If you are seriously interested in having an Australian Cattle Dog puppy of the quality to show or to breed, wait with your selection until the puppy is at least five to six months old. By this time, you can be far more certain of dentition, soundness, and attitude, as well as other important characteristics. No matter what you have in mind for your dog's future—dog shows, Cattle Dog, or nothing more than loving companionship—all of the foregoing should be considered carefully and, above all, temperament of the puppy and of its

The Australian Cattle Dog puppy you select should be a happy, playful extrovert.

parents must be a paramount factor in deciding which Australian Cattle Dog to take home.

If the excitement and pride of owning a winning show dog appeals to you, we strongly urge you to seek out a successful breeder who has a record of having produced winning dogs through the years. As stated, it is extremely difficult, if not impossible, to predict what an eight-week-old puppy will look like as an adult. An experienced breeder, however, will know whether a young puppy has "potential." Unfortunately, most prospective owners want both a very young puppy and some guarantee that the puppy will grow up to be a winning show dog but it is not possible to give that kind of guarantee, and no honest breeder will do so.

Show-prospect Puppies

A show-prospect puppy must not only adhere to all the health and soundness qualifications of the good pet puppy, it must show every sign that it will conform very closely to the rigid demands of the breed standard (see pages 14–17) when it matures. It might make little difference to you if your pet is a bit longer in body or shorter on leg than the ideal set up in the breed standard but faults like this make considerable difference in determining the future of a show dog.

All male show dogs must have two normal-sized testicles in the scrotum. Some males have only one testicle, which eliminates them from being considered as a show prospect. Certainly this would make no difference to pet owners who will have their male dog sexually altered anyway; therefore, purchasing a male with this "fault" could give the buyer a beautiful dog that is not otherwise affordable.

Your chances of obtaining an Australian Cattle Dog puppy that will mature into a winning adult are far better if purchased from a breeder whose bloodline has produced many champions. Even at that, no one can be sure of having a winner until the puppy has reached maturity. Obviously, a puppy that is six or seven months old, or a young adult will provide much more certainty.

We have known some people who have spent thousands of dollars buying very young puppies again and again but have never achieved their goal of owning a winning show dog. Granted, an older puppy or grown dog may initially cost considerably more than an eight-week-old puppy, but odds are much greater that in the end you will have what you actually wanted.

Experienced and successful Australian Cattle Dog breeders have spent years developing a line of top-quality animals. These breeders know what to look for in the breed and they are particularly familiar with the manner in which their own stock matures.

Price

The price of an Australian Cattle Dog puppy can vary considerably but it should be understood that reputable breeders have invested considerable time, skill, and work in making sure they have the best possible breeding stock, all of which costs a great deal of money. Good breeders have also invested substantially in veterinary supervision and testing to keep their stock as free from hereditary defects as possible.

A puppy purchased from an established and successful breeder may cost a few dollars more initially, but the small additional investment can save many trips to the veterinarian over the ensuing years. It is heartbreaking to become attached to a dog only to lose it at an early age because of some health defect.

You should expect to pay $500 or more for an eight-week-old, pet-quality Australian Cattle Dog puppy. Older puppies will cost more. Youngsters with show and breeding potential may be double that price and young show stock that has reached the five- or six-month-old stage will be even more expensive.

Veterinary Health Check

A responsible breeder will be more than happy to supply a written agreement that the sale of a puppy is contingent upon the puppy's successfully passing a veterinary health check. If the location of the breeders, your home, and your prospective veterinarian allow it, plan the time of day you pick up your puppy so that you can go directly from the breeder to the veterinarian. If this is not possible, you should plan the visit as soon as possible. No longer than 24 hours should elapse before this is done. Should the puppy not pass the veterinary health check, a responsible and ethical breeder will be more than happy either to refund your money or provide you with another puppy depending on the stipulations of the contract.

What You Must Get with Your New Puppy

Inoculations and Health Certificates

By twelve weeks of age most puppies have been vaccinated against hepatitis, leptospirosis, distemper, parainfluenza, and canine parvovirus. Rabies inoculations are usually given at four months of age but some states have regulations requiring this be done as early as twelve weeks if the puppy is being sold. There is a set series of inoculations developed to combat these and other infectious diseases and more details are given in the chapter Medical Problems, beginning on page 77.

You are entitled to have a record of these inoculations when you purchase your puppy.

Most breeders will give you complete documentation, along with dates on which your puppy was wormed and examined by the veterinarian. Usually, this record will also indicate when booster shots are required. These are very important records to keep safe—they will be needed by the veterinarian you choose to care for your Australian Cattle Dog.

Pedigree and Registration Certificate

Buying a purebred dog also entitles you to a copy of the dog's pedigree and registration certificate. These are two separate documents. The former is simply the dog's family tree and lists the registered names of your Australian Cattle Dog's sire and dam along with their ancestors for several generations.

The registration certificate is issued by the American Kennel Club. When ownership of your Cattle Dog is transferred from the breeder's name to your name, the transaction is entered on this certificate, and, once mailed to the AKC, it is permanently recorded in their computerized records. The AKC will send you a copy of the duly recorded change. File this document in a safe place along with your other important papers, as you will need it should you ever wish to show or breed your Australian Cattle Dog.

It is important to understand that the pedigree is simply a listing of the dog's ancestors. The fact that a dog has a pedigree means only that it is purebred, that all of its ancestors are, in fact, Australian Cattle Dogs. The pedigree does not mean a dog is of superior or show quality. All of the dogs in the pedigree could have been of strictly pet quality. On the other hand, the pedigree could just as well be made up of Australian Cattle Dogs that have won many show ring titles.

Diet Sheet

A sound and healthy Australian Cattle Dog puppy is in that condition because it has been properly fed and cared for. Every breeder has a slightly different approach to successful nutrition, so it is wise to obtain a written record or description that details the amount and kind of food your puppy has been receiving. It should also indicate the number of times a day your puppy has been accustomed to being fed and the kind of vitamin supplementation it has been receiving. Maintaining this system at least for the first week or two after your puppy comes home with you will reduce the chances of digestive upsets and loose stools. A good diet program also projects increases in food and changes that should be made in the dog's diet as it matures.

Consider an Adult Dog

A very young puppy is not your only option for adding an Australian Cattle Dog to your household. For some people, especially the elderly, a housebroken adult can be an excellent choice. Also, if time available to housebreak is limited, or the owner expects to be away from home frequently, an adult Cattle Dog can be a wise choice.

If, in fact, your Australian Cattle Dog will be a working Cattle Dog, buying a young adult or even one fully matured that has been trained may be just the answer. A trained Cattle Dog knows what it has been taught and will perform well for a new owner so long as the new owner has learned how to give commands properly.

There are some important things to consider in bringing an adult Australian Cattle Dog into your home:

✔ The adult dog may have developed habits that you do not find acceptable. In some cases it may be difficult to retrain such animals. Until you begin to work together, there is no way of knowing how willing an adult Australian Cattle Dog is to learn new habits. Always take an adult dog home on a trial basis to see how it works out for both you and the dog.

✔ Another factor to consider is that some adult Australian Cattle Dogs may never have been exposed to or interacted with small children. If there are young children in your home, the first sight of these "miniature people" can be very perplexing to the inexperienced Australian Cattle Dog, especially loud and very active children. When children run and play, the herding and heeling instinct in the dog may be aroused; perhaps leading to nipping at the children's feet and ankles. It may take considerable time and patience to overcome this inborn instinct but with perseverance and good judgment most Cattle Dogs can be retrained.

Importance of a Training Regimen

The Australian Cattle Dog was bred to do a job and in order for it to learn to do its job, it had to inherit a capacity to be trained. Many animal behaviorists place the Australian Cattle Dog among the most trainable and versatile of all the canine breeds. While certainly a great asset when properly channeled, this capacity left untapped can result in an extremely trouble-some, often neurotic dog. The prospective Cattle Dog owner must be totally committed to establishing and regularly following a training regimen with the dog he or she buys.

Basic obedience training is not a matter of choice in Australian Cattle Dog ownership—it is a matter of absolute necessity. Anyone who is not willing to invest the time and effort to provide his or her Australian Cattle Dog with the training it needs should really look to another breed. It makes no more sense to own a dog with a great capacity to work and learn and have it lie idly about than it would to own a high-performance race car that is used only to drive a block or two to the market once a week.

There is no question as to the trainability and intelligence of the Australian Cattle Dog. The only question that remains is the owner's willingness and ability to provide the proper training and environment.

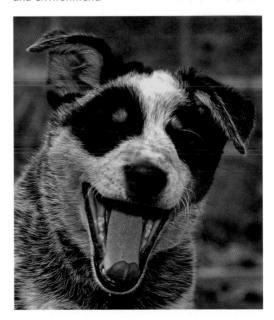

Responsible breeders are happy to give a written statement to the effect that the final sale of their puppies relies on a successful veterinary health examination.

Early Training

Simple basic training should begin just as soon as you bring your puppy home. It must be remembered, however, that a young puppy's attention span is very short and puppies are incapable of understanding or retaining complex commands.

It should also be noted here that as rugged a breed as the Australian Cattle Dog is, it is very sensitive to correction and a stern scolding is usually sufficient to get your point across. Striking an Australian Cattle Dog (or any other dog) is never necessary; in fact, it is apt to have exactly the opposite effect intended. There are occasions when you may have to take sterner measures but they can normally be taken care of by grabbing your dog by the ruff on both sides of the neck just behind the head and giving the dog a very firm and sharp *"No!"*

Learning the Meaning of "No!"

Probably the most important single command your dog will ever learn is the word *"No!"* Never use the word unless you are prepared to enforce it. This is the only way the puppy will understand its meaning, and once understood, it can and will save both you and the puppy a great deal of unnecessary trauma.

The very first time your puppy nips at someone's heels (including your own), you must correct the puppy with a very firm "No!" The Australian Cattle Dog has a barely suppressible urge to bite at heels and while this may be cute behavior for an eight-week-old puppy, it is downright dangerous for an adult Australian Cattle Dog to do this. Puppy growling and biting falls under the same heading. Do not let it get started. As with all unwanted behavior in dog training, avoidance is more than half the battle.

The Come Command

The next most important lesson for the puppy to learn is to come when called. It is critical, therefore, that the puppy become familiar with its name as soon as possible. Learning to come when called could well save your dog's life when the two of you venture out into the world. *Come,* the command a dog must understand, has to be obeyed always and instantly, but the dog should not associate that command with fear. The dog's responding to its name and the word *Come* should always be associated with a pleasant experience such as great praise and petting or a food treat.

In dog training of any kind it is much easier to avoid the establishment of bad habits than it is to correct entrenched, undesirable behavior. Never give the *Come* command unless you are sure your puppy will come to you. Initially, use the

There are times when stern measures are necessary to correct bad habits. When this occurs, hold your Australian Cattle Dog by the ruff on both sides of the neck, just behind the head, and give a very firm "No!"

command when the puppy is already on its way to you or give the command while walking away from the youngster.

Very young puppies will normally want to stay as close to their owner as possible, especially in strange surroundings. When your puppy sees you moving away, its natural inclination will be to get close to you. This is a perfect time to use the *Come* command.

Later, as the puppy grows more independent and perhaps a bit headstrong, you may want to attach a long leash or rope to the puppy's collar to insure the correct response. Chasing or punishing your puppy for not obeying the *Come* command in the initial training stages makes the youngster associate the command with something negative and will result in avoidance rather than the immediate positive response you desire. It is imperative that you praise your puppy when it does come to you, even if it delays responding for many minutes.

Leash Training

It is never too early to accustom the puppy to a collar and leash; it is your way of keeping your dog under control. It may not be necessary for the puppy or adult dog to wear its collar and identification tags within the confines of your home and property, but no dog should ever leave home without a collar and without the leash held securely in your hand.

✔ Begin getting your puppy accustomed to its collar by leaving it on for a few minutes at a time. Gradually extend the time you leave the collar on. Most puppies become accustomed to their collar very quickly and forget they are even wearing it.

✔ Once this is accomplished, attach a light-weight leash to the collar while you are playing

When attempting to accustom your puppy to the collar and leash do not guide the youngster at first. The point is just to familiarize him to the feeling of wearing the collar and leash.

with the puppy in the house or in your yard. Do not try to guide the puppy at first. The point here is to accustom the puppy to the feeling of having something attached to the collar.

✔ Encourage the puppy to follow you as you move away. Should it be reluctant to cooperate, coax it along with a treat of some kind. Hold the treat in front of the puppy's nose to encourage it to follow you. As soon as the puppy takes a few steps toward you, praise it enthusiastically and continue to do so as you move along.

✔ Make the initial session very brief and very enjoyable. Continue the lessons in your home or yard until the puppy is completely unconcerned about the fact that it is on a leash. With a treat in one hand and the leash in the other you can begin to use both to guide the puppy in the direction you wish to go.

✔ Once the collar and leash are accepted you can begin your walks near to the house and eventually around the block. You and your Australian Cattle Dog puppy are on your way to a lifetime of adventure together.

CARE OF THE AUSTRALIAN CATTLE DOG PUPPY

There is a great deal you can do prior to your puppy's arrival to make the transition painless and trauma-free. If possible, visit your puppy several times while it is still in its original home so that you are not entirely a stranger.

Preparing for the New Puppy

Well in advance of the puppy's arrival you can secure the equipment and toys that will be needed and prepare the area in which it will initially live. A fenced-off area in the kitchen is the ideal place to start your puppy off; accidents can be easily cleaned up and the kitchen is a room in which there is normally a good deal of traffic. Don't forget, a young puppy is accustomed to the companionship of its littermates, and without them the puppy will be lonely. It will be up to you to compensate for the loss of your puppy's siblings.

Preparing ahead of time will help the Australian Cattle Dog puppy to become a member of its new human family.

Equipment and Toys

The following is a list of the basic requirements you should already have satisfied when your puppy arrives. The value and use of each will be more fully explained as we proceed.

Partitioned–off living area: Paneled fence partitions about four feet (122 cm) high are available at most major pet shops and are well worth the investment for keeping the puppy where you want it to be. Australian Cattle Dog puppies love to be where their owners are but puppies should not be underfoot.

Cage or shipping kennel: Inside the fenced-off area there should be a wire cage or fiberglass shipping kennel (the open door of which provides access to a sleeping "den"). This cage will also be used for housebreaking (see page 42). These wire cages and fiberglass shipping kennels come in varying sizes. The number

400 size, which is approximately 36 inches (92 cm) long by 24 inches (61 cm) wide by 26 inches (66 cm) high, will be the ideal size to accommodate an Australian Cattle Dog through adulthood.

Water dish and feeding bowl: These are available in many different materials. Choose something nonbreakable and not easy to tip over—Australian Cattle Dog puppies very quickly learn to upset the water bowl and relish turning their entire living area into a swimming pool! We recommend stainless steel bowls as they eliminate the worry of toxic content of some plastics and are not as easily chewed and destroyed.

Food recommended on the "diet sheet": In the unlikely circumstance that you were not provided with this information by the puppy's breeder, there are many highly nutritious commercial brands of dog food available at pet stores and supermarkets that come complete with feeding instructions. Veterinarians are always helpful in this area as well.

Brush and comb: A young Australian Cattle Dog's coat does not require a great deal of grooming, but grooming is important and the process should begin early. Equipment that you will need is described in detail in the chapter

When selecting feed and water bowls, always choose something nonbreakable and sturdy.

Bathing, Grooming, and Home Health Care beginning on page 67.

Soft collar and a leash: There are soft fabric collars that weigh next to nothing that can be purchased at any pet shop. These are ideal for the beginning lessons in that a collar of this type can barely be felt when it is around the puppy's neck. Lightweight plastic or fabric leashes are good for the young puppy because they will not weigh heavily on the puppy's neck.

Toys: These can be anything you choose, but be sure they are safe—without buttons or strings that can be chewed off or swallowed. The Australian Cattle Dog has incredible strength in its jaws, even as a puppy, and can easily demolish things other dogs cannot! Also, avoid hard plastic toys that can splinter. Make sure all toys are larger than those that the puppy can get into its mouth; small toys can become lodged in the mouth and caught in the throat. Do not give your Cattle Dog puppy old and discarded shoes or socks to play with. A puppy is unable to determine the difference between "old" and "new" and unless carefully watched may think it is perfectly all right to add newly acquired dancing slippers to its toy collection.

Be prepared in advance of the puppy's arrival. A small fenced-off area in the kitchen will avoid a host of problems.

Bringing Your Puppy Home

The safest way to transport the puppy from the kennel to your home is to obtain a pet carrier or cardboard box large enough for the puppy to stretch out comfortably with sides that are high enough so that it cannot climb out. Put a layer of newspapers at the bottom in case of accidents and a soft blanket or towel on top of that. Ideally, another family member or friend should accompany you to do the driving or hold the carrier that the puppy is in.

Helpful hint: When your puppy arrives at its new home it will be confused and undoubtedly whine in search of its littermates, especially at night when its littermates are not there to snuggle up to. For the first few nights after the new puppy arrives, we put a box next to the bed and let the newcomer sleep there. Should the puppy wake up crying in loneliness, a reassuring hand can be dropped down into the box and we have avoided having to trudge to a different part of the house to quiet the lonely puppy.

Letting the puppy "howl it out" can be a nerve-racking experience that could easily cost you, your family, and your neighbors nights of sleep. Should you wish to transfer the puppy's sleeping quarters to a different part of the house later, you can do this more easily once the puppy has learned to be by itself for increasing periods of time.

"Puppy-Proofing" Your Home

A good part of your puppy's safety depends upon your ability to properly "puppy-proof" your home. Electrical outlets, lamp cords, strings, and mouth-size objects of any kind all spell danger to the inquisitive puppy. If you think of your new

Even the Australian Cattle Dog puppy has incredible strength in its jaws and can easily demolish things other dogs cannot.

arrival as equal parts building inspector, vacuum cleaner, and demolition expert you will be better equipped to protect your puppy.

Australian Cattle Dog puppies can be ingenious at getting into places they shouldn't be.

Toys for the Australian Cattle Dog puppy should be chosen carefully. They should never have buttons or strings that can be chewed off or swallowed. Rope toys and Kong chew toys are ideal for the Cattle Dog puppy.

Leaving its littermates can be very bewildering to the new puppy. It will be up to the owner to compensate for the puppy's siblings.

Things like household cleaning products, gardening supplies, and poisonous plants should be kept in securely latched cupboards or well above a puppy's reach. Most veterinarians will be able to supply you with a list of plants that are poisonous to dogs.

There is a product called Bitter Apple that tastes just like it sounds—*terrible!* Actually a furniture cream, it is nonpoisonous and can be used to coat electrical wires and chair legs. In most (not all) cases, it will deter your puppy from damaging not only household items but itself as well. Should Bitter Apple not work, there is plastic tubing available at hardware stores that can be put around electrical cords and some furniture legs. Still, a bored and restless Australian Cattle Dog puppy can chew through plastic tubing quicker than most of us are capable of putting it down, so never underestimate the ability of your puppy to get into mischief!

There are baby gates to keep your puppy out and cages and kennels of various kinds to keep your puppy in. All this and a daily "Puppy-proofing Patrol" will help you and your pet avoid serious damage and potential danger.

Lifting and Carrying Your Puppy

Learning to pick up and carry the very young Cattle Dog puppy properly is very important for both adult and child. You should pick up the puppy with one hand supporting its rear and hindquarters and the other hand under the puppy's chest. This gives the puppy a feeling of security and enables you to keep full control. A puppy should *never* be picked up by its front legs or by the scruff of the neck.

Only children old enough to safely hold and control a puppy should be allowed to pick it up. Australian Cattle Dog puppies are very strong for their size and can suddenly squirm and attempt to jump down out of a child's arms. A fall from any height can seriously and permanently injure a puppy.

The New Puppy and Other Pets

The Australian Cattle Dog puppy's introduction to older and/or larger dogs in the household must also be carefully supervised. The average Cattle Dog puppy loves the world and all creatures in it; however, even at a very early age it is inclined to be a little bossy. The adult dog "with seniority" may consider the new youngster an intrusion and mistake its exuberance for aggression. For this reason it is very important to confine the newcomer so that the older dog is not

Even though the Cattle Dog puppy loves the world and all creatures in it the youngster can be a little bossy with other, even older, animals.

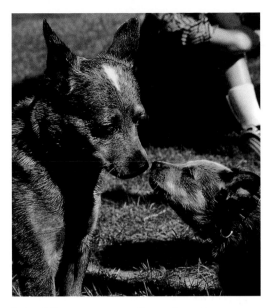

constantly harassed before it has had time to fully accept the puppy. The partitioned area set up to accommodate the new puppy that we described earlier will give the senior member of the canine contingent an opportunity to inspect the new arrival at his or her leisure without having to endure unsolicited attention.

Given their "druther's" an Australian Cattle Dog prefers to be the only canine on its premises. On the other hand, many Cattle Dog owners tell of their dogs getting along famously with resident dogs, cats, even other small animals— even to the point of appointing themselves guardians and protectors.

The Chase Instinct

Australian Cattle Dogs are the wonderful herding dogs they are because they have an extremely elevated prey drive. This instinct makes *anything* that moves fair game, including bicycles, lawn mowers, cars, skateboards, and even vacuum cleaners. Owners report that cats that stand their ground are apt to do well with an Australian Cattle Dog, but cats that run are not apt to fare as well.

Car Travel

A part of an Australian Cattle Dog puppy's socialization process will take place away from home. The puppy must learn to accept strange people and places, and the only way for the puppy to learn to take these changes in stride

is to visit as many new sites and meet as many strangers as you can arrange. Trips to the shopping mall or walks through the park will expose your young Cattle Dog to new and different situations each time you are out. Of course this should never be attempted until your puppy has had all of its inoculations. Once that is completed, you are both ready to set off to meet the world and this often involves riding in a car.

Most adult Australian Cattle Dogs love to ride in a car. The moment they hear those car keys jingle they are ready and willing to go. Some puppies, however, unfortunately suffer varying degrees of motion sickness. The best way to overcome this problem, should it exist, is to begin with very short rides, such as once around the block. Ending the ride with a fun romp, or a little food treat, helps make the ride something to be enjoyed. The puppy should not be fed a full meal before the ride.

A Cattle Dog should never leave home without a collar and identification tag.

When the puppy seems to accept these short rides happily, the length of time in the car can be increased gradually until you see that the puppy is truly enjoying the outings. Even those dogs and puppies suffering the most severe cases of car-sickness seem to respond to this approach and soon begin to consider the car a second home.

Words of Caution on Dogs and Cars

As much as it might seem more enjoyable to have your Australian Cattle Dog puppy or adult ride loose in the car, this can be extremely dangerous. An overly enthusiastic canine passenger can interfere with the driver's control or divert the driver's attention. Also, a sudden stop can hurl your dog against the front window, severely injuring or even killing it.

The safest way to transport your Cattle Dog is in a carrier with the door securely latched. There are also cars such as station wagons that accommodate partitions commonly referred to as "dog guards." These safety devices confine dogs to the rear portion of the car. Employing these simple safety precautions might one day save the life of your pet.

Tags: Another important travel tip is to make sure your canine companion is wearing a collar with identification tags attached. In fact, when-ever your Cattle Dog is not at home with you, it should be wearing a collar with identification tags. Many times, a dog is thrown clear of the car in an accident but becomes so frightened that it runs blindly away. Not knowing where it is and not carrying any means of identification, the dog may be lost forever.

Closed windows: It is probably best to avoid leaving your dog alone in a car at anytime. However, if you must leave your dog alone, make it a practice to keep the windows at least partially open. Even on cool days the sun beating down on a closed car can send the inside temperature soaring. Leaving an Australian Cattle Dog alone in an unventilated car could easily cause its death.

Housebreaking

Previously we mentioned the great value in getting your Australian Cattle Dog accustomed to a wire cage or fiberglass shipping kennel. These containers are commonly called crates by dog breeders and are invaluable in housebreaking your dog.

It has been our experience that new dog owners will initially look upon the crate method of confinement during housebreaking as cruel, but more often than not, these same people come back to thank us for suggesting the crate method as one of the most valuable training tips they have ever learned. Using a crate reduces the average housebreaking time to a minimum and eliminates keeping the puppy under constant stress by correcting it for making mistakes in the home. Most dogs, and Australian Cattle Dogs in particular, continue to use their crates voluntarily as a place to sleep, as it provides a sense of safety and security. It becomes their cave or den and in many cases a place to store their favorite toys or bones.

Those of us who live in an earthquake-prone area find our dogs will make a hasty retreat to their crate at the earliest sign of a tremor. Often we have found it necessary to become very persistent in order to get some dogs to emerge from their crate even after the quake has long passed.

Confining your dog is the only possible way to avoid having soiling accidents in the house. Australian Cattle Dogs are instinctively clean animals and will not soil their immediate surroundings unless they have no choice.

The Crate Method

The crate used for housebreaking should not be too large or the puppy will sleep at one end and eliminate in the other. It should be large enough for the puppy to stretch out comfortably as well as stand up and turn around easily. Naturally, this creates a problem, as the proper size crate for an eight-week-old puppy will not be the proper size for a six-month-old puppy. The easiest way to solve this is to use a piece of plywood to block off a part of the crate, adjusting the space accordingly as the puppy grows.

Feeding in the Crate

Begin using the crate by feeding the puppy in it. Close and latch the door while the puppy is eating. As soon as the food has been consumed, unlatch the crate door and *carry* the puppy outdoors to the place where you want it to eliminate. Should you not have access to the

The ticking of an alarm clock under a blanket in the new puppy's bed will duplicate the heartbeat of its missing littermates.

The ideally sized kennel for the adult Australian Cattle Dog is one that can be partitioned off to accommodate the needs of a puppy.

outdoors, or feel you will later not be able to provide outdoor access for the housebroken dog, place newspapers or some other absorbent material in an out-of-the-way place that will remain easily accessible to the dog. Do *not* let the puppy run around or play after eating until you have carried it to the designated area. It is extremely difficult to teach a puppy not to eliminate indoors once it has begun to do so; therefore, it is very important to prevent accidents rather than correct them.

The Australian Cattle Dog is not a breed that can be deprived of human companionship. Constant human interaction brings the breed's capabilities to their peak.

Being Consistent

Young puppies will void both bowel and bladder almost immediately after eating, after strenuous play, and upon waking from a night's sleep or even a nap. Being aware of this will save a good many accidents. If, after each of these activities, you consistently take the puppy to the place designated for eliminating, you will reinforce the habit of going there for that purpose.

Only after seeing that the puppy has relieved itself in both ways should you allow the puppy to play unconfined and then only while you are there to watch what is happening. Should the puppy begin to sniff the floor and circle

When to Take Your Puppy Outdoors
- Very first thing in the morning.
- Immediately after eating.
- Immediately after drinking.
- Right after a nap.
- When it circles and sniffs the floor.
- Right after playtime.
- When it gets that "perplexed," anxious look.
- When it starts to squat.

around or squat down to relieve itself, say *"No!,"* pick it up immediately, and take it to the designated place.

When you are not able to watch what the puppy is doing indoors, it should be in the crate with the door latched. Each time you take the puppy to its crate, throw a small food treat into the crate and praise the puppy as it enters the crate to go after the treat. If the puppy starts whining, barking, or scratching at the door because it wants to be let out, it is crucial that you do not submit to those demands. The puppy must learn not only to stay in its crate, but also to do so without complaining unnecessarily.

Every time the puppy begins to whine or bark say *"No!"* very firmly. If necessary, give the crate a sharp rap with a rolled-up newspaper. It may take a good bit of persistence on your part, but patience will win out in the end.

Developing a Schedule

It is important to realize that a puppy of eight to twelve weeks will have to relieve its bladder every few hours except at night; therefore, you must adjust your schedule and the puppy's accordingly. You must also be sure your puppy has entirely relieved itself at night just before you retire and be prepared to attend to this the very first thing in the morning when you awake. How early in the morning your puppy needs its first outing will undoubtedly be determined by the puppy itself, but do not expect the young puppy to wait very long for you to respond to its "I have to go out now" signals. You will quickly learn to identify the difference between a puppy's signals that nature is calling and those that indicate it simply does not want to be confined.

Care and persistence in this project pays off very quickly with practically all Australian Cattle Dog puppies, and eventually you will begin to detect a somewhat anxious look or attitude in the puppy that indicates that it needs to relieve itself. Even the slightest indication in this direction should be met with immediate action on your part and accompanied with high praise and positive reinforcement.

When the Owner Is Away

The crate method of housebreaking is without a doubt the simplest and quickest method I have ever found to housebreak a puppy. It is obvious, however, that this method cannot be used if you must be away from home all day or for even many hours at a time. Everyone has an occasional day away from home but if these prolonged absences are to occur daily, the Cattle Dog puppy is not the ideal "home alone" candidate. We repeat—the Australian Cattle Dog was bred to work and to be with its owner. Neither of its basic needs can be fulfilled living in a home where the dog's owner is absent day in and day out. Serious emotional problems can result.

Again, we must stress that young puppies cannot contain themselves for long periods of time. If the puppy must regularly be left alone for more than two or three hours at most, an alternative method must be used, but confinement is still the operative word for success.

For obvious safety reasons, an Australian Cattle Dog puppy should never be left to roam the house while the owners are away. It is dangerous for the puppy and accidents are bound to happen. The fenced-off area in the kitchen recommended for the arrival of the new puppy is the ideal place of confinement for your puppy while you are gone. The space should be only large enough to permit the puppy to eliminate away from the place in which it sleeps. The entire kitchen area is normally too large a space and creates the eliminating at random habit that is to be avoided at all cost.

The floor of the fenced-off area should be lined with newspaper. The puppy will become accustomed to relieving itself on the newspaper and this should become the "designated spot" to which you will take your puppy when you are home and the puppy indicates it has need to eliminate. When you are home, you must insist the puppy use the newspapers every time.

The Australian Cattle Dog puppy will follow bouts of play with a well-deserved nap.

The Unique Cattle Dog

There is little doubt that the Australian Cattle Dog is a unique and wonderful breed—rugged, alert, sensitive, independent, and able to think for himself. However, those same exceptional qualities can present a host of problems for the new owner who is not aware of just how to handle this lusty product of Australia's outback.

Left to his own devises the Australian Cattle Dog is apt to make all kinds of decisions on his own—who he will like, or will not, who should be protected and with what degree of aggressiveness, who belongs and who does not. All of these things that may be considered cute in young puppies are definitely not so in an adult. In fact, left unchecked, decisions of this nature can be worrisome to the owner and others, if not downright dangerous.

The new Cattle Dog owner must never forget that the breed was developed to have the courage and determination to take on a full-grown, half-wild steer. That's a lot of courage and determination to have running around unharnessed. Furthermore, once an Australian Cattle Dog learns something, it can be hard to change his mind. Putting oneself in charge from the very beginning is critical and socialization essential.

Good Cattle Dog breeders make it a point to expose their puppies to as many everyday sights, sounds, and strangers as possible, but this is not always practical when there are many dogs to be taken care of. Therefore, it is up to you to gently and gradually introduce your puppy to as many unaccustomed events and people as you are able. This is not a matter of choice; it is one of necessity.

Young Children

Regardless of whether the Cattle Dog puppy has had prior experience with young children, the children themselves must be educated about what they may and may not do with the new puppy. Learning the gentle approach and exercising caution when the puppy is underfoot are things all children should know.

In the case of an Australian Cattle Dog puppy, children must understand that no "puppy bites" are allowed under any condition, nor should they encourage the puppy to chase them in fun. Cattle Dog puppies should never be allowed to bite for any reason. Breaking the habit is extremely difficult. Cattle Dogs have an inborn desire to chase and nip at heels—again, cute as puppies, extremely dangerous as adults.

The puppy must also be taught to get on well with

It is important to educate children as to what they may and may not do with the new puppy.

your children's playmates. Roughhousing can be a difficult thing for the adult Cattle Dogs to understand. It ignites their innate protective mechanism and could easily result in a Cattle Dog biting to protect its young charge.

Note: Children must understand that once the Australian Cattle Dog puppy enters the home there can never be any "fun" puppy biting or chasing games.

Meeting Strangers

Take your new Cattle Dog puppy with you to as many places as you possibly can. This is perfectly safe once the puppy has had all required inoculations. Having the puppy meet as many new humans and dogs as possible is critical to your dog's socialization.

Children should never be allowed to encourage playful "puppy bites" or to allow the puppy to chase them in fun. These behaviors are extremely difficult to correct as the puppy grows up.

Give everyone who likes dogs the opportunity to pet your puppy and don't ignore any attempts the youngster makes to avoid meeting new friends. Should your puppy give any indication of shying away from the attention of a stranger, pick the puppy up and hold him securely to give him confidence, and then let the new person continue making gestures of friendship. Make a habit of carrying little treats with you and hand one to the stranger to give to the puppy. The way to a puppy's heart can be through a tasty treat.

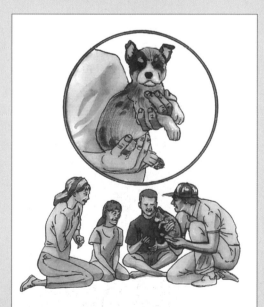

Everyone in the family must learn how to properly pick up and carry the puppy.

CARE OF THE ADULT AUSTRALIAN CATTLE DOG

Most owners are quick to agree that failure to provide an Australian Cattle Dog with something to do will definitely inspire it to become quite creative on its own. That creativity, unfortunately, might prove terribly costly to the negligent owner and the Cattle Dog's determined nature will not have that behavior easily dissuaded.

Prepare for an Active Dog

There are some breeds that do well living outdoors in a run or in a kennel with only minimal human contact. There are others that are perfectly content to lounge on the sofa all day while their owners are away from morning to night. Rest assured, the Australian Cattle Dog is neither! Its entire genetic makeup urges it to be continually active both mentally and physically. If you as an owner accommodate this activity, you will have a dog that will at times amaze you with its intelligence and readiness to learn. If you do not work with your Australian Cattle Dog there is little doubt that behavioral problems will develop.

Helpful hint: Plan on giving your Australian Cattle Dog time to "work." That work can take the form of allowing your dog to perform its obedience repertoire, playing flyball or frisbee,

Learning commands comes very quickly to the Australian Cattle Dog.

or perfecting its agility or herding exercises. These activities are described in greater detail in the chapter titled, Sharing Your Life with an Australian Cattle Dog, beginning on page 85. This, combined with daily walks, grooming sessions, and simply having your Australian Cattle Dog sit beside you while you watch television or read will satisfy your dog's need for activity and human contact.

Outdoor Manners

Since a good part of the time you spend with your Cattle Dog will be outdoors, consideration must be given to keeping your dog under control at all times. As previously stated, always use a leash and collar and make sure the identification tags are securely attached to the collar.

Use of a leash is particularly important when your Cattle Dog will be near children. Young children are high-energy individuals and there is no way nor any need to keep them from running and being noisy. This will awaken every herding instinct an uncontrolled Cattle Dog possesses and the unrestrained dog could well run off herding the children and biting at their heels.

An Australian Cattle Dog may not be inherently quarrelsome but it will not take aggression on the part of another dog lightly. You must have your dog under control at all times, even though other people may not be equally responsible.

Never let your dog relieve itself where people might walk or children are playing. Try to teach it to use the gutter to relieve itself. Even then, you should always carry a small plastic bag to remove droppings immediately and dispose of them in a trash receptacle. Many city governments impose heavy fines on dog owners who do not pick up after their dogs.

Dealing with Behavior Problems

Most of the behavior problems owners experience with their Australian Cattle Dogs are due to the fault of the owner rather than the dog. One must not forget that an Australian Cattle Dog is first and foremost a dog, and one of the basic needs of all dogs is to have a "pack leader." A

pack leader sets boundaries and in so doing gives the members of the pack a sense of security.

Boundary setting and enforcing those boundaries do not intimidate your dog or diminish its capacity to learn. Setting limits actually establishes a line of communication between you and your dog that works for both of you.

Protective and Aggressive Tendencies

An Australian Cattle Dog will protect its owner and its owner's property at the cost of its own life if need be. This is an admirable quality but here again, unchecked, this tendency can lead to an Australian Cattle Dog deciding on its own what and how it will protect. Obedience training and an unquestioned willingness to respond to the *No* command are an absolutely necessary part of your dog's education. An Australian Cattle Dog must understand when and from whom it should protect you; it must understand that *protection does not include aggression!*

Chewing

Puppies will chew. It helps them through their teething stages, and it exercises and strengthens their jaws. Dogs chew things because they enjoy it. Chewing relieves stress and boredom. Your dog must learn early on what it can and cannot chew. Half the battle is in preventing dogs from chewing the wrong things. Don't give your dog the opportunity to do so.

A dog cannot tell the difference between your discarded old slipper and your newest pair of

If your puppy is confined to its crate while you are unable to keep your eye on it, there will be less chance of the youngster using your valuables as play toys to relieve the need to chew.

The Australian Cattle Dog's high energy level requires constant exercise.

dress shoes; both smell exactly like you and are just as chewable. Don't expect your dog to understand that it is acceptable to chew on one and not the other. Never give your dog any of your personal items to chew on; you must assist the dog's learning that none of the smell-just-like-you items is a plaything.

Make sure your Australian Cattle Dog is confined to its crate or dog-proof room with something it is allowed to chew when you are not there to supervise. Sound cruel? Think again. Which is more cruel—safely confining your dog when you are not there or flying into a rage because the dog entertained itself by eating a hole in the sofa while you were gone?

Housebreaking Problems

Housebreaking is based upon a dog's natural dislike for eliminating where it eats and sleeps. An Australian Cattle Dog is a particularly clean dog but supervision is important in having the dog understand human cleanliness rules. A dog does not have to eliminate near its food or sleeping place when given freedom of the whole house. For more on housebreaking, see page 42.

Jumping Up

Even people who like dogs do not particularly enjoy being jumped up on when they enter someone's home. Consistency is the only thing that works here. Do not let your dog jump up on your leg or on anyone else's—ever. A leg is a leg, and if it is acceptable to jump up on yours for a pat, then in the dog's mind all other legs are fair game as well.

When your Australian Cattle Dog runs joyfully to greet you and jumps up for a pat, give the command *Off!* and push its paws off your leg. As soon as the dog's paws hit the floor, praise it lavishly. Everyone in the family must do this or it will not work. When you and your dog are away from home, have your dog under control on its leash and repeat the command when your dog attempts to jump up on strangers.

Refusing to Stay "Home Alone"

The Australian Cattle Dog is a social creature and some of them become more upset at being left alone than others. Some dogs may bark, whine, or attempt to destroy things. All dogs must learn that your absence is simply a matter

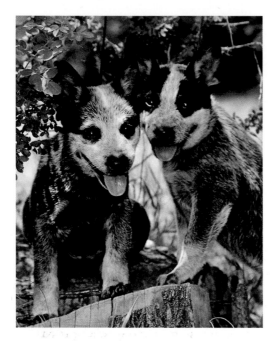

Everything in the Cattle Dog's genetic makeup urges it to be busy and involved in some form of work. If the owner accommodates this need the dog will amaze with its intelligence and readiness to learn.

plish with some dogs than it does with others, but persistence is the key. When being left alone is no longer a traumatic experience, you can experiment with leaving the dog loose in a room or in the house if you wish, but again, this should be done gradually.

Digging

All dogs like to dig. Australian Cattle Dogs love it! They do it to relieve boredom and to find a nice cool spot to lie in. They do it to seek and destroy vermin they know (or think they know) are hidden under the ground. Correcting the digging problem is not easy.

Again, supervision works best. If it is not possible to supervise your dog while it is outdoors, keep it inside until you can be there to watch what is going on. The minute your dog attempts to dig, let it know with that tried-and-true *No* command that this is not acceptable. Good luck on this one!

Some Cattle Dog owners have dealt with the digging problem by providing their dogs with a place to do just that. A pit at the back of one's property or in the corner of the yard can be allocated for its digging needs, and with patience and supervision dogs can be trained to understand that their "pit" is the only place digging is allowed. You can encourage your dog to dig in its own pit by burying some delectable "treasures" there. Once or twice, assist the dog in finding what is buried there and give lavish praise when the objects are "found."

of routine. Don't treat your departure or return like the climax in a romance novel. Dogs get caught up in your emotional responses. If the dog relates your coming and going with hugging, kissing, and all kinds of heightened emotion, anxiety sets in.

Feeling secure in the kennel or cage you have provided is the first step in your Australian Cattle Dog's "home alone" training. This nips in the bud any chance of destructive behavior. Going in and out of the room while the dog is confined is the next stage. The dog is learning that you do come back.

Stepping outside the house but remaining within earshot comes next. The minute the barking or howling begins, you must command *No!* Increase the time you are out of sight but not out of earshot. Eventually, your absence will go by unnoticed. This may take longer to accom-

Spaying and Neutering

All companion Australian Cattle Dogs, whether male or female, should be sexually altered unless specifically purchased to breed or to show. Only an Australian Cattle Dog purchased from a breeder who has recommended that it be bred should be allowed to have offspring. You would be astounded by how many dogs and cats, numbering in the millions, are put to sleep each year because they have no homes.

We trust that you, as a responsible dog owner, would never allow your Australian Cattle Dog to roam the streets, nor would you consider turning it over to the dog pound. Yet there is no way you can guarantee that someone who might purchase a puppy from you will not be irresponsible and permit the dog to roam or wind up being euthanized at the pound.

Parents who wish to have their young children "experience the miracle of birth" can do so by renting videos of animals giving birth. Handling the experience this way saves adding to pet overpopulation.

There is constant lobbying throughout America to restrict the rights of all dog owners and dog breeders because of this pet overpopulation and the unending need to destroy unwanted animals. Thoughtful dog owners will leave the breeding process to experienced individuals who have the facilities to keep all resulting offspring on their premises until suitable and responsible homes can be found for them.

Altering your pet can also avoid some of the more distasteful aspects of dog ownership. As previously discussed, males that have not been altered have the natural instinct to lift their legs and urinate on objects to mark the territory in which they live. It can be extremely difficult to teach an unaltered male not to do this in your home. Unaltered males also have a greater tendency to roam if there is a female in heat in the area. Veterinarians advise that neutering will also help to prevent perianal tumors and prostate cancer in males.

The female will have two estrus cycles each year that are accompanied by a bloody discharge. Unless the female is kept confined, there will be extensive soiling of the area in which she is allowed and, much more disastrous, she could become mismated and pregnant. Unspayed females also have a much higher risk of developing pyometra or mammary cancer later in life.

Toys

The rules governing the selection of toys for an Australian Cattle Dog puppy apply throughout the lifetime of your dog. Never give an Australian Cattle Dog a toy that is small enough to fit in the dog's mouth or that can be chewed apart into small pieces. Extra consideration must be given to the Cattle Dog's phenomenal jaw power. A toy that might last some other breed a lifetime can be shattered in minutes by the Australian Cattle Dog. Very strong rubber rings and toys designed for large dogs are usually suitable for the Australian Cattle Dog.

Some Cattle Dogs treasure teddy bears and other stuffed animals and keep them nearly intact for many years; however, in most cases toys of this kind can be dangerous. More than one dog has expressed its displeasure at being left behind by completely dismantling a favorite teddy bear or stuffed doll. The danger here is that the material with which the toy has been stuffed can be ingested and cause severe illness or even death.

Training classes are especially good for the Australian Cattle Dog because they provide an opportunity for the dog to understand that commands must be obeyed even when strange people are present.

Bones

Bones of any kind are not a wise choice for an Australian Cattle Dog. They can even splinter large knucklebones. Further, if there are any traces of meat on the bone, there is a breeding ground for bacteria and if the bone remains outside, it can attract vermin.

Instilling Good Behavior

Responsible owners will have begun training when their Cattle Dog arrived (see pages 34–35). Trying to undo bad habits is extremely difficult with any dog and particularly so with this headstrong breed. For instance, a dog that has been permitted to sleep on its owner's bed or climb up on furniture for many months can simply not understand why, starting today, this is no longer allowed.

You may well have a good reason for making this change, but you will be hard-pressed to make your Australian Cattle Dog understand this reason. What will result instead is a constant war; your Cattle Dog will do everything in its power to resume its comfortable habit, and you will lose patience with its attempts to do so. If your dog's first attempts to break any household rule are met by your firmly grasping it by the ruff of the neck and a sharp *No!* it is highly unlikely the issue will become a contest of wills.

You need not worry about hurting the dog's feelings so long as you are not unfair, inconsistent, or violent. Aggression on the part of your Australian Cattle Dog should not be tolerated; avoid allowing it ever to start. Do not permit your puppy ever to growl or snap should you want to take away a toy or pick up its food dish. If you allow this behavior when your dog is a youngster, you can rest assured you will wind up with an Australian Cattle Dog that will challenge you at every turn as an adult. A sharp rap with your fingers on the nose of the puppy that is testing its dominance by growling or biting will not have any ill affects upon its development. It will, however, go a long way in preventing a dangerous problem from ever getting under way.

An Australian Cattle Dog cannot be bullied. It will simply not respond to that kind of treatment. Clear consistent rules are what the breed needs and thrives on.

Training Classes

For obedience work beyond the basics described, it can be extremely beneficial for the Australian Cattle Dog owner to seek out local professional assistance. This can be obtained in many ways. There are free-of-charge classes at Department of Parks and Recreation facilities, as well as very formal and sometimes very expensive individual lessons with private trainers. There are some obedience schools that will take your dog and train it for you; however, we find in the case of Australian Cattle Dogs that there is no substitute for the rapport that develops when dog and owner train together.

Training classes are especially good for Australian Cattle Dogs because they give them an opportunity to learn to respond in the midst of strange dogs and strange people. The classes are also a wonderful socialization opportunity for the dogs.

Traveling with Your Dog

At first thought, having your Cattle Dog accompany you on an extended trip may sound like great fun for both of you, but further consideration could well alter your decision:

✔ You must ask yourself where your Australian Cattle Dog will stay when you stop along the way to eat or to sleep. Unlike most European countries, restaurants in America do not permit dogs to accompany their owners inside the establishment.

✔ Leaving your dog in a parked automobile while you eat can be very dangerous, as weather conditions can change rapidly and temperatures in a closed car can soar.

✔ Leaving the windows open puts your pet in danger of escaping or being stolen, even if it is safely secured in a traveling container. A slightly open window is of little help once the sun begins to beat down on the car.

✔ Many hotels and motels do not allow dogs into the rooms because other guests have abused this privilege in the past. Many of the hotels and motels that do allow pets into the rooms charge an extra fee or security deposit. These establishments also assume that your dog is accustomed to being left alone in a strange place and will not disturb other guests by barking and howling while you are out of your room.

✔ Changing your dog's accustomed food and water can create a number of problems, including diarrhea, not something most people wish to cope with while traveling.

Have a Good Trip

It should be easy to see that taking your Australian Cattle Dog along with you on a trip will require a great deal of advance planning. An air-conditioned car can help considerably if your trip will be made through areas where daytime temperatures are high. Take the crate or cage with you that you have been using at home. This keeps your pet safe while traveling and provides a safe, secure, and familiar place for the dog if you are out of your hotel room.

Stops along the way must be carefully planned. Realize that your selection of restaurants will have to be made with your pet's safety in mind. At any stop your car must not be left in the sun. Further, unless the weather is very cool, windows should be left open if your dog is in a cage or crate and your car must be where you or a member of your party can see it at all times.

Many people who travel with their pets make an early morning stop at a grocery store or carry-out restaurant and purchase their own food for the day. Meal stops can then be made at some shady spot along the way. Should you decide to do this, it will also give you an opportunity to exercise your dog at the same time.

Dinnertime should come after you have checked into your hotel or motel and put your dog in your room. Reservations must be made in advance with those places that allow dogs in the rooms. If you have taken our previous advice and trained your Australian Cattle Dog to stay alone in its kennel or cage, you will not have to worry about barking and howling while you are gone, nor will you run the risk of having your dog cause any damage to the room.

Leaving your dog alone: If you have not accustomed your dog to being left alone in its kennel, it is to be hoped that it has at least learned to be left alone. If so, we seriously advise closing your Australian Cattle Dog in the bathroom while you are out of the room. It is very important to leave a "Do not disturb" sign on your door while you are gone to avoid a staff person's entering your room. An Australian Cattle Dog considers guarding your temporary accommodations from intrusion just as important as guarding your regular home.

If your dog will not stay alone in a strange room without barking, *do not leave it!* The dog can become frenzied and destroy things or disturb the other occupants of the hotel.

Food and water: You must take along an adequate supply of your Australian Cattle Dog's accustomed food and water. Changing diets and water can seriously upset your dog, and diarrhea and vomiting are the last things you will want to deal with in your hotel room.

Brush and comb: Do take your dog's brush and comb along. If you plan to hike or walk your dog along the side of the road, these accessories will enable you to get rid of any unwanted weeds, seeds, or dirt your Australian Cattle Dog's coat might have attracted.

Alternatives to Traveling with Touser

There are many excellent boarding kennels located around most towns and cities that offer facilities that will satisfy the needs of both you and your dog. Speak to your veterinarian, friends, or clients who are familiar with the boarding operation before leaving your dog.

Should you be convinced that your dog could never be happy in a boarding kennel, there are responsible, bonded, and experienced "pet sitters" who will come to your home and stay with your pet while you are away. Your veterinarian may be able to supply you with the names of individuals who are experienced at providing this kind of service. It is always wise to ask for references from the individuals who provide this service and important that the references be checked out thoroughly.

Your Aging Dog

The Australian Cattle Dog ages remarkably well, and though lifespan does vary from dog to dog, it is not unusual to find many members of this breed alive and active even at 12 and 14 years of age.

Exercise

There are certain precautions that must be taken with the older Australian Cattle Dog to keep it happy and healthy. Exercise must be adjusted as your dog gets older and you must take pains to see that it is not pushed beyond its capacity when hiking or playing.

Diet

Your Australian Cattle Dog's diet must also be adjusted accordingly so that there is less strain on the digestive system. The fat content of the

Many Australian Cattle Dogs are alive and active at 12, even 14 years of age, and they often retain their sight, hearing, and all their teeth until their final days.

food must be reduced. Today, most major dog food manufacturers take canine aging into consideration and offer diets specifically geared to the senior citizen. Your veterinarian can advise you about which diets to choose.

If your Australian Cattle Dog has been accustomed to one major meal each day it is probably wise to adjust this to two or three smaller meals. It is also absolutely necessary to avoid overweight in the aging dog. The strain of additional weight will certainly shorten its lifespan.

Health Problems

Aging frequently affects the Australian Cattle Dog's ability to see and hear. If you find your previously obedient Cattle Dog is failing to respond quickly or not at all to your call, do make concessions for age, but be sure to have your dog checked out by the veterinarian for seeing or hearing problems.

Also, the old Australian Cattle Dog's patience may wear thin much more quickly than it did when it was a youngster. Puppies and children can prove extremely tiresome to the elderly Cattle Dog and it is up to the owner not to allow the old-timer to be subjected to youthful harassment.

Excessive drinking of water can be a sign that the kidneys are not working properly. In some cases this can be a sign that bitches that have not been spayed are developing pyometra, which is an inflammation of the womb, a condition that requires prompt professional treatment.

Veterinary science has developed many new methods that assist your dog to stay healthy even through its final years. Regular checkups will prevent rapid progress of the ailments that could lead to the deterioration of your pet.

The Last Good-bye

There will come a time when your canine friend of many years is no longer able to enjoy life and you must make a very painful decision. Fortunately, when science is no longer able to prevent our pets' suffering or incontinence, we are able to mercifully bring their lives to a close.

Your veterinarian will tell you when the time has come to do this and is able to perform this final act with tenderness and skill. Done professionally, there is no stress to your dog, especially if you are there to hold the dog while the veterinarian administers the injection.

This is never an easy decision to make but carefully considered, it is the kindest action you can take for your canine companion that has given you so many years of love and enjoyment.

FEEDING

There is no simple way to answer the question of what is the best food to give your Australian Cattle Dog. Probably, the best answer to the question is, "Feed what works best for the dog." I strongly recommend consulting the breeder from whom you purchased your dog, as well as your veterinarian.

Your Australian Cattle Dog can be put on an adult feeding schedule at about ten months of age. This means it will receive one main meal a day, preferably at the same time each evening. This meal is supplemented by a morning snack and for this we highly recommend hard dog biscuits made for large dogs (remember those powerful jaws!). These not only prove to be a much anticipated treat, but do wonders toward maintaining healthy gums and teeth.

Amount to Feed

The correct amount of food to maintain an Australian Cattle Dog's optimum condition varies as much from dog to dog as it does from human to human. It is impossible to state any

Proper nutrition and exercise will help the Australian Cattle Dog avoid becoming overweight.

specific *amount* of food your dog should be given. Much depends upon how much your dog exercises. An Australian Cattle Dog that spends the entire day working cattle will need considerably more food than the house dog whose exercise is limited to 20 or 30 minutes a day retrieving a ball.

Generally speaking, the amount of food for a normally active Cattle Dog is the amount it will eat readily within about 15 minutes of being given the meal. What your dog does not eat in that amount of time should be taken up and discarded. Leaving food out for extended periods of time can lead to erratic and finicky eating habits.

It must be remembered that the Australian Cattle Dog was originally bred to be a working Cattle Dog. Meals were sporadic, of questionable nutritious value, and came only after a long, grueling day's work. Today's dog has every bit as big an appetite as its ancestors but usually has

Hard dog biscuits made for large dogs are excellent for maintaining healthy gums and teeth and are highly anticipated treats for the Australian Cattle Dog.

far less work to do. The breed can gain weight very easily if not watched and not given a considerable amount of exercise.

A good rule of thumb to follow in determining whether or not an Australian Cattle Dog is receiving the proper amount of food is closely monitoring the dog's condition. You should be able to feel the ribs and backbone through a slight layer of muscle and fat.

Essential Nutrients

Fresh water and a properly prepared balanced diet containing the essential nutrients in correct proportions is all a healthy dog needs to be offered. If your Australian Cattle Dog will not eat the food offered, it is because it is either not hungry or ill. If the former is the case, the dog will eat when it is hungry. If you suspect the latter, an appointment with your veterinarian is in order.

Dogs, whether Australian Cattle Dogs or Chihuahuas, are carnivorous (meat-eating) animals, and while the vegetable content of your dog's diet should not be overlooked, a dog's physiology and anatomy are based upon carnivorous food acquisition. Protein and fat are absolutely essential in a dog's diet. The animal protein and fat your dog needs can be replaced by some vegetable proteins, but the amounts and the kind require a better understanding of nutrition than most people have.

There are so many excellent commercial dog foods available today that it seems a waste of time, effort, and money to try to duplicate the nutritional content of these carefully thought-out products by cooking food from scratch. It is important though that you read labels carefully or consult with your veterinarian, who will assist you in selecting the best moist or dry food for your Australian Cattle Dog.

Canned Food or Dry?

A great deal of research is conducted by manufacturers of the leading brands of dog food to determine the exact ratio of vitamins and minerals necessary to maintain your dog's well-being. Research teams have determined the ideal balance of minerals, protein, carbohydrates, and trace elements for a dog's well being. Dog food manufacturing has become so sophisticated it is now possible to buy food for dogs living almost any lifestyle, from sedentary to highly active. This applies to both canned and dry foods, but like most other things in life, "you get what you pay for." It costs the manufacturer more to produce a nutritionally balanced, high-quality food that is easily digested by a dog than it does to produce a brand that provides only marginal nourishment.

By law, all dog food must list all the ingredients in descending order by weight. The major ingredient is listed first, the next most prominent follows, and so on down the line.

A diet based on meat or poultry (appearing first in the ingredients list) is going to provide more nutrition per pound of food than one that lists a filler grain product as the major ingredient. The diet based on meat and poultry will also cost more than a food heavy in inexpensive fillers.

Whether canned or dry, look for a food in which the main ingredient is derived from meat, poultry, or fish. Remember, you cannot purchase a top-quality dog food for the same price as one that lacks the nutritional value you are looking for. In many cases you will find your Australian Cattle Dog not only needs less of the better food, but there will be less fecal waste as well.

The Appearance of Dog Food

The better foods are not normally manufactured to resemble products that appeal to humans. A dog does not care that a food looks like a sirloin steak or a wedge of cheese—all a dog cares about is how food smells and tastes. The "looks like" dog foods are manufactured to tempt the dog's owner, but since it is highly unlikely that you will be eating your dog's food, do not waste your money.

Be aware of canned or moist products that have the look of "rich red beef," or dry food that is red in color. In most cases, the color is put there to appeal to you and is achieved through the use of red dye. Dyes and chemical preservatives are no better for your dog than they are for you. A good red dye test is to place a small amount of canned or well-moistened dry food on a piece of white paper towel. Let the food sit there for about a half hour and then check to see if the towel has been stained. If the toweling has taken on a red stain, you can rest assured the color is there to appeal to your eye and not your dog's.

In nature the pack leader eats first.
Your dog should be fed after you
and your family have eaten.

Special Diets

A good number of dog-food manufacturers now produce special diets for overweight, underweight, and older dogs. While the amount of these foods that one should feed may remain the same as standard products, the calorie content is adjusted to suit the particular problem that accompanies each of these conditions.

There is no better remedy for these conditions, however, than using good, common sense. Obviously, too many calories and too little exercise will increase weight; fewer calories and an increase in physical activity reduces weight.

The geriatric or overweight dog needs a much lower-calorie diet than the growing puppy or adult dog of normal weight. It is also important to make sure your older dog get its fair share of exercise each day. The old-timer may prefer to spend more of its day on the sofa than when it was a youngster, but moderate exercise even for the very old dog will keep your friend alive much longer.

TEACHING COMMANDS

Australian Cattle Dogs have been bred to respond to force with force. Thus teaching puppies is a critical part of early training. There are several different methods, but the key is consistency. Pick a method and work with it. Most of all, you need to make sure that you are communicating with your dog.

The adaptability or resistance to training of individual Australian Cattle Dogs runs the gamut from "I love doing this" to "Don't push me!" It will be up to you to determine just where your dog falls along this spectrum. Most dogs of the breed understand very quickly, but just as many will perform more readily when they feel that they are doing so because it is their own idea. Therefore positive reinforcement works best. That is, praising an Australian Cattle Dog for doing something right is far more effective in getting your point across than forcing a behavior and sternly correcting them when they don't respond to your satisfaction. The latter is apt to cause resentment and resistance.

It is very important that training begins early with the Australian Cattle Dog.

The Sit Command

Commonly, dog owners attempt to teach the *Sit* command by pushing down on the dog's hindquarters while giving the command. A far better technique for teaching the Australian Cattle Dog this command is to begin with a hungry puppy who will pay close attention to you and the treats you are using.

While standing or kneeling in front of your puppy, let him see that you are holding the treat. Touch the treat to your puppy's nose and give the command *Sit*, using the puppy's name— *"Sit, Blue, Sit!"* Do so using a cheerful tone of voice.

If you move the treat back over your dog's head he will invariably move backward and sit. Keep repeating this action and the command until he does. Once your puppy sits give him tons of praise and the small treat. "Good boy Blue, good boy!"

Once the sit lesson has been mastered, you can start on the stay command.

Keep repeating this process until your dog does sit. Then, and only then, comes the praise and the treat. Most puppies are apt to try and jump up for the treat, but if you continue the nose to back of head routine the *sit* message will eventually get through.

The Stay Command

Repetition is the key here. Once you see that your puppy has connected your *Sit!* command and the motion of your hand to what he must do, you can begin the *Stay!* command. Continue to use the same hand motion even after your puppy has learned to sit when you use just the verbal *Sit!* command without a treat.

Make the *Sit!* command a game and use it throughout the day, eliminating the treat when the command alone gets the desired response. However, continue the lavish praise.

Have your Cattle Dog sit next to your left side and hold a treat in your right hand a good distance from his nose and give the *Stay!* command. If your dog attempts to get up to go after the treat, put your left hand on his chest, which should keep him in the *sit* position, repeating *Stay!* Even a few seconds of staying should be rewarded with a treat and lots of praise and then

an *Okay*, which is the sign that he can get up. This will take some repetition but eventually your dog will make the connection and you can extend the stay time before giving the *Okay* and treat.

Once your dog begins to understand what it must do, you can gradually increase the distance you step away. Your Australian Cattle Dog eventually must learn that the *Sit, Stay* commands must be obeyed no matter how far away you are. Later, with advanced training, your dog will learn that the command is obeyed even when you move completely out of sight.

Once your dog has remained in the *sit* position for as long as you have dictated, do not call it to you. This makes the dog overly anxious to get up and run to you. Instead, walk back to the dog and repeat the *Okay* that is a signal the command is over. Later, when your dog becomes more reliable in this respect, you can call it to you.

The *Sit, Stay* lesson can take considerable time and patience with some dogs but usually the Australian Cattle Dog understands very quickly and, once understood, has little problem in demonstrating its newly acquired lesson.

We reserve at least the *stay* part of the training until an Australian Cattle Dog is at least six months old because everything in a very young puppy's makeup dictates that, for protection, it get up and follow you wherever you go.

Down

Once your dog has mastered the *Sit* and *Stay* commands, you may begin work on *Down*. This is especially useful if you want your dog to remain in a particular place for a long period of time. *Down* is the one word command for *lie down*. *Down* must only be used when you want the dog to lie down. If you want your dog to get down from the sofa or to stop jumping on you, use the *Off* command.

Have your dog sit next to your left side and kneel down beside him. Hold a treat in your right hand and rest your left hand lightly on his rear. Put the treat under his nose and move your hand down to the floor. Keeping your hand gently on his rear will encourage him to slide down to get at the treat. While doing this say, *"Down Blue, down!"* Always use a pleasant tone. You don't want your dog to feel he is being reprimanded or punished.

Be patient. You may have to repeat this process a number of times before your dog gets the fact that *Down!* means getting those elbows down on the ground. However, the minute that he does do so—the treat and loads of praise!

Heel

One of the best methods I have found to accustom a dog to the heeling exercise was learned from a friend and longtime breeder of Australian Cattle Dogs. It is especially effective for young puppies. She uses a straightened coat hanger, the tip of which is bent back on itself to create a loop. It is there she fastens a soft or sticky treat. She begins with the dog sitting at her left side with her left hand on the leash shortened to the extent that she can maintain direct contact with the dog without pulling. She holds the remainder of the leash in her right hand along with the non-treat end of the coat hanger.

She then begins walking at a rate that keeps the dog moving forward at her side rather than leaping in the air for the treat. While she is doing so, she gives the *Heel!* command. When the dog has taken a number of steps forward

Teaching your dog to heel not only makes your walks more enjoyable, it is the very basis for off-leash control.

she stops, gives the *Sit!* command and then the treat with lots of praise. Her left hand on the leash enables her to give some gentle guidance. Eventually the dog becomes accustomed to being close to her left side as they move along, knowing that if he does so, the treat and/or praise will come.

The training collar and leash: I have found a lightweight, link-chain training collar to be very useful, particularly for the heeling lesson. It provides slight pressure around the neck and a jangling sound, both of which get the dog's attention. Erroneously referred to as a "choke collar," the link-chain collar used properly will not choke the dog.

As soon as your dog has learned to walk along on the leash, guide him to walk on your left side. A quick short pressure on the leash will keep your dog from lunging from side to side, pulling ahead, or lagging back. Always keep the leash slack while your dog maintains the proper position at your side. Should the dog begin to drift away, give the *heel* command, followed immediately by a light jerk on the leash, and guide the dog back to the correct position.

Do not pull on the leash with steady pressure. All you need to get your dog's attention is a gentle jerking motion.

BATHING, GROOMING, AND HOME HEALTH CARE

Your Australian Cattle Dog will not require much of your time or equipment in the way of grooming, but that is not to say that it needs no care at all in this respect. While the Australian Cattle Dog's coat may be referred to as "wash and wear," regular brushing keeps the coat clean, odor-free, and healthy.

Equipment Needed

Most Australian Cattle Dogs will shed their coats twice a year. However, the Cattle Dog is what is referred to as a "double-coated" breed. The undercoat is short, soft, and dense. It acts as a weatherproofing blanket. The outer or top coat is longer and harsher and therefore more protective. To say that the breed sheds is an understatement. Their twice yearly shedding leaves clouds of hair everywhere, indoors and out. The Cattle Dog will also drop the longer guard hairs almost all year-round.

As a result, regular grooming sessions year-round are absolutely necessary to both assist the shedding process and to keep the person assigned house-cleaning chores from being driven to distraction.

Regular grooming of the Australian Cattle Dog will help prevent minor health problems from becoming more serious.

Regular grooming gives you the opportunity to keep on top of your dog's home health care needs. Such things as clipping nails, cleaning ears, and checking teeth can be taken care of during the time set aside for grooming.

Grooming table: Investing in a grooming table that has a non-slip top and an arm and noose can make all of these activities infinitely easier. These tables are available at pet shops and it is important to choose a table with a height that allows you to stand or sit comfortably while you are working on your dog. We use a grooming table that has an "arm" and a "noose." The noose slips around the dog's neck when it is standing and keeps the dog from fidgeting about or deciding it has had enough grooming.

Do not attempt to groom or attend to your dog's health care while you and your dog are sitting on the floor. You will spend most of your time chasing the dog around the room and Australian Cattle Dogs, particularly, will simply

Use a grooming table that has an "arm" and a "noose." This keeps the dog from fidgeting about or deciding that it has had enough grooming. However, never leave the dog alone on a grooming table.

wander off when they feel they have had enough of your attention.

Brushes, combs, clippers: Invest in a good stiff bristle or wire brush, a steel comb, and animal nail clippers. You will be using this equipment for many years so buy the best equipment that you can afford.

Brushing

Undoubtedly, the breeder from whom you purchased your Australian Cattle Dog will have begun to accustom the puppy to grooming just as soon as there was enough hair to brush. You must continue with grooming sessions or begin them at once if for some reason they have not been started. It is imperative that you both learn

to cooperate in this endeavor in order to make it an easy and pleasant experience.

Brush with the lay of the hair and use the steel comb on the longer hair of the "pants" on the dog's rear legs and on the tail. At shedding time there will be a tremendous amount of hair collected in your brush and comb. You can hasten this process by giving your Cattle Dog a warm bath once the shedding has begun. This loosens the hair and, though you may think your dog will complete the process completely bald, fear not— once the dead coat has been removed, the shedding stops and new hair growth will begin.

Nail Trimming and Foot Care

This is a good time to accustom your Australian Cattle Dog to having its nails trimmed and having its feet inspected. Always inspect your dog's feet for cracked pads. Check between the toes for splinters and thorns, paying particular attention to any swollen or tender areas. In many sections of the country there is a weed that has a barbed hooklike affair that carries its seed. This hook easily finds its way

Always brush your Australian Cattle Dog with the lay of the hair, starting at the head and working vigorously back toward the tail.

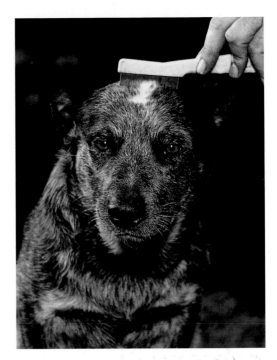

into a dog's foot or between its toes and very quickly works its way deep into the dog's flesh, causing soreness and infection. These barbs are best removed by your veterinarian before serious problems result.

We suggest attending to your dog's nails every other week. The nails of an Australian Cattle Dog that spends most of its time indoors or on grass when outdoors can grow long very quickly. Do not allow the nails to become overgrown and then expect to cut them back easily. Each nail has a blood vessel running through the center called the "quick." The quick grows close to the end of the nail and contains very sensitive nerve endings. If the nail is allowed to grow too long it will be impossible to cut it back to a proper length without cutting into the quick. This causes severe pain to the dog and can also result in a great deal of bleeding that can be very difficult to stop.

If your Cattle Dog is getting plenty of exercise on cement or rough hard pavement, the nails may stay sufficiently worn down; otherwise, the nails can grow long very quickly. They must then be trimmed with canine nail clippers, an electric nail grinder (also called a drummel), or coarse file made expressly for that purpose.

The Australian Cattle Dog's dark nails make it practically impossible to see where the quick ends, so regardless of which nail trimming device

is used, you must proceed with caution and remove only a small portion of the nail at a time.

Should the quick be nipped in the trimming process, there are any number of blood-clotting products available at pet shops that will almost immediately stem the flow of blood. It is wise to have one of these products on hand in case your dog breaks a nail in some way.

Every dog's nail has a blood vessel that runs through the center, called the "quick." The quick grows close to the end of the nail and contains very sensitive nerve endings.

Bathing

Dog show exhibitors use coat care products that adhere to the Cattle Dog's hair and most exhibitors bathe their dogs before shows. Even at that, some exhibitors do use "dry bath" products rather than the tub and shampoo method. Well-kept Australian Cattle Dogs are literally odor-free and frequent bathing is unnecessary.

When your Cattle Dog does require a wet bath, you will need to gather the necessary equipment ahead of time. A rubber mat should

Nail care must begin in puppyhood. Starting too late can result in being met with great resistance.

be placed at the bottom of the tub to keep your dog from slipping and thereby becoming frightened. A rubber spray hose is absolutely necessary to thoroughly wet the coat. It is also necessary to remove all shampoo residue.

A small cotton ball placed inside each ear will prevent water from running down into the dog's ear canal. Be very careful when washing around the eyes as soaps and shampoos can be extremely irritating.

It is best to use a shampoo designed especially for dogs; the pH balance is adjusted to keep drying to a minimum and leaves the hair shining and lustrous.

Technique

In bathing, start behind the ears and work back. Use a washcloth to apply the soap, and rinse around the head and face. Once you have shampooed your dog, you must rinse the coat thoroughly and when you feel quite certain all shampoo residue has been removed, rinse once more. Shampoo residue in the coat is sure to dry the hair and could cause skin irritation.

As soon as you have completed the bath, use heavy towels to remove as much of the excess water as possible. Your dog will assist you in the process by shaking a great deal of the water out of its coat on its own.

Always use a shampoo specifically designed for dogs. The pH of these products is adjusted to keep the dog's hair shiny and lustrous.

Home Health Care

It is important to establish a weekly health care routine for your Australian Cattle Dog. Maintaining this schedule will prevent escalation of serious problems that may take expensive veterinary attention.

Eye care: If the eyes are inflamed or discharging any kind of matter, check for foreign bodies such as soot or weed seeds. Regular flushing of the eye with cotton and cool water will help relieve the eye of debris and pollen. If your dog's eyes water continuously, have your veterinarian inspect them for a condition called entropion, in which the eyelid is inverted and the eyelashes cause irritation to the eye. It can be corrected by surgery. Entropion is very rare in Australian Cattle Dogs but has been reported in some instances.

Ear cleaning: The insides of the ears should always be clean and pink. Nothing other than a cotton Q-tip should ever be inserted into the ear itself and never probe into the inner recess of the ear. Use the Q-tip moistened with olive or almond oil to clean the ear. If wax has accumulated, dip the Q-tip into rubbing alcohol, squeeze out the excess thoroughly, and clean out the ear.

Do not attempt to treat an ear that has an unpleasant odor. Consult your veterinarian immediately. The odor may indicate the presence of parasites in the ear, or worse, there may be an ear infection.

Anal sacs: The anal sacs (also referred to as the anal *glands* by many breeders) are located on each side of the anus and should be regularly looked after. They can become blocked, causing extreme irritation and abscesses in advanced cases.

If you notice your Australian Cattle Dog pulling itself along the ground when it is sitting down, you should check the anal glands. While

Regular brushing assists greatly in keeping your dog's teeth clean and free of dental plaque.

not a particularly pleasant part of keeping your dog healthy, if regularly attended to, keeping the anal glands clear is relatively easy.

The best time to attend to this job is when you are giving your dog its bath. With the dog in the tub, place the thumb and forefinger of one hand on either side of the anal passage and exert pressure. The glands will empty quickly. Wear rubber gloves when performing this function and it is best to cover the anus itself with a cotton swab or tissue. Should you be unsure of how to perform this procedure, your veterinarian or the breeder from whom you purchased your Australian Cattle Dog will instruct you.

Dental care: Care should always be given to the state of your dog's teeth. If your dog has been accustomed to chewing hard dog biscuits or gnawing on large rawhide bones since puppy-

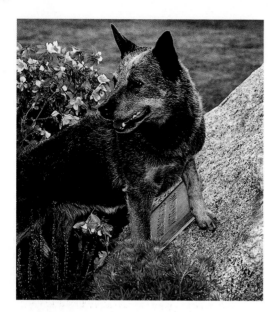

As diligent as you might be about caring for your Cattle Dog and keeping the coat in good condition, you must be aware that fleas lurk everywhere and are a problem with which you need to deal.

hood, it is unlikely that you will have any problems as this chewing activity assists greatly in removing dental plaque, which is the major cause of tooth decay. Any sign of redness of the gums or tooth decay merits expert attention.

Retention of baby teeth can cause long-term problems with the permanent teeth. Generally, by the time the permanent teeth have come through at about five months of age, the baby teeth have all fallen out. If there are any baby teeth remaining at this stage, seek your veterinarian's advice on their removal. Retaining baby teeth can interfere with the proper placement of your Australian Cattle Dog's permanent teeth.

Parasites

Fleas: Adult fleas are about 1/8 inch long, wingless, and have three pairs of legs. The hind pair of legs is modified for jumping. Fleas are vertically flat like a fish, and can move easily through the hair of a host. The immature stage or larval stage of the flea looks like a small white worm with a dark head. Flea eggs are small and white.

Adult female fleas require a blood meal to produce viable eggs. Eggs are laid on the dog, but because they are not glued onto hairs, the eggs fall off the animal into the bedding, carpet, yard, or wherever a dog spends most of its time. It has been recorded that a single female flea may lay 400–800 eggs over the span of five months! The very small, worm-like larvae live among the carpet fibers or cracks and crevices in the home. Adult fleas emerge from the cocoon very quickly and immediately jump on the host. Once on the host they feed on blood by biting through the skin. Given the best conditions, a flea can go through its entire life cycle in 14 days.

While fleas are a problem everywhere, these pests can be especially troublesome for those who live in climates that have no freezing temperatures to kill off the existing infestation. Granted, the flea force returns just as soon as the warmer weather sets in, but at least there is some respite. The more temperate climates do not even have this relief.

As fastidious as you might be about caring for your Australian Cattle Dog and keeping its coat in good condition, you must be aware that fleas will still be a problem unless dealt with on a continuing basis. Even if you were to protect your Cattle Dog like a hothouse flower, daily walks can bring fleas into your home, and

Even healthy puppies like this should see their veterinarian for regular checkups.

once there the little creatures multiply with alarming rapidity.

Flea shampoos, powders, and sprays that were customarily used in the past contain insecticides that vary in their effectiveness. Their goal was to remove the fleas that were present on the animal at the time of use, thus constant repetition was necessary. But even then the products failed significantly to rid the household or dogs' living quarters of the problem.

According to *Consumer Reports'* August 1991 edition, flea collars aren't effective and are probably a waste of money. Ultrasonic flea collars are absolutely worthless because they do not work.

Fortunately there are significant advances that have been made in the last decade or so to safely and effectively control flea infestation. Not all require veterinarian prescription, but it is always wise to consult your veterinarian on the advisability and dosage of any of these products and always read and follow label directions for the safe use of any pesticide.

The University of Ohio conducted extensive research on modern flea control products and found several very effective:

Lufenuron (Program) is produced by Novartis Animal Health. It offers complete flea prevention for the entire season by treating your dog monthly beginning in early spring, before the flea season starts. For dogs that live in kennels or warm climates, year-round treatment may be recommended. The product is formulated as a pill for dogs. This flea control medication is only available from a veterinarian. It effectively sterilizes the female flea by preventing eggs from hatching. Data shows that within seven days after lufenuron is fed to the animal, virtually 100 percent of the eggs laid by female fleas failed to hatch. Novartis Animal Health states that the product is also safe for breeding and lactating animals. All cats and dogs in a household must be treated with lufenuron because any untreated animals can infest your household with fleas.

The only way to keep your Australian Cattle Dog happy and healthy is to be sure that external and internal parasites are taken care of before they become a problem.

Fipronil (Frontline) is a Rhone Merieux product. Frontline kills fleas for up to three months on dogs; ticks are also killed for a month or more. According to Rhone Merieux, Frontline Top Spot can be used on puppies as young as ten weeks old. A premeasured dosage in a plastic pipette is applied to the skin in a spot between the pet's shoulder blades. Fipronil collects in the oil-producing glands of the skin and wicks back out with the fur for up to three months. The product is so effective that it is not removed by bathing or swimming.

Imidacloprid (Advantage) is produced by the Bayer company. The active ingredient in this product kills adult fleas on contact before they can lay eggs. Advantage is applied to the skin over the back, and then diffuses through the skin over the rest of the body. The treatment works quickly; 98–100 percent of adult fleas are killed within 24 hours after application. A single dose lasts approximately one month on dogs. To prevent fleas, this product should be applied monthly. Because Advantage is not systemically absorbed, the product is considered to be very safe.

Treating the Home: Although the products listed immediately affect the fleas existing on your dog, it is important to take effective steps against the larvae living in the bedding and carpeting of your home and in any outside living quarters, if they exist. Washing bedding in hot water and thoroughly vacuuming carpets should kill the larval fleas as well as the organic matter that the larvae feed on. There are also insecticide spray treatments that can be used to reduce the number of existing adult fleas.

Nature's way: Many people dislike using chemical toxins of any kind on or around themselves or their dogs. A number of natural products are in use that reportedly are effective in flea control and elimination.

When ingested by a dog, brewer's yeast gives an odor that repels fleas. Citronella is another product that has an odor that fleas dislike. Other products made from citrus oils are said to paralyze the flea's respiratory system.

It is always best to consult a veterinarian for help in fighting the flea battle. He or she knows which products are most effective in the immediate area and they are inclined to keep abreast of new developments in combating the problem.

Fleas act as carriers of the tapeworm's eggs. When a dog swallows a flea, the tapeworm eggs grow in the dog's intestines. Tapeworms are discussed under the heading Internal Parasites on page 81.

Lice: Lice are seldom a problem with the well-cared for Australian Cattle Dog, because the pests are spread by direct contact. In other words, to have lice your dog must spend time with another animal that has lice or be groomed with a contaminated brush or comb. Since these pests are minute in size, they are not as easy to see as fleas.

If no fleas are present and you suspect lice, the dog must be bathed with an insecticidal shampoo every week until the problem is eliminated. Fortunately, unlike fleas, lice live and breed entirely on the dog, so it is not necessary to treat the entire area in which the dog lives.

Ear mites: Ear mites are parasites that settle in the external ear canal. They can lead to chronic irritation. Symptoms are an extremely disagreeable odor, a dark waxy secretion, and constant scratching at the ear by the dog. Once present, ear mites can be extremely persistent, particularly if a dog becomes severely infested. Flushing of the ear by a veterinarian is recommended.

Ticks: Your Cattle Dog can pick up ticks by running through grass, wooded areas, or even through sand at the beach. Ticks are bloodsucking insects that bury their heads firmly into the skin. They can become a source of extreme irritation to your dog and can cause secondary infections as well. It is important to loosen the tick's grip before you attempt to remove it; otherwise, you may allow the head to break away from the tick and remain lodged in the dog's skin. This also can create severe infections.

To remove adult ticks, soak them with a spray made especially for tick removal; once the parasite has loosened its grip, you can remove it with a pair of tweezers. Regular bathing with a tick dip will prevent reinfestation but, as is the case with all dips and sprays, read the instructions carefully as some of these products may be toxic.

The entire environment in which the dog lives must be regularly and vigorously treated against ticks especially if you live adjacent to a wooded area or beach. Ticks can transmit serious diseases that can endanger humans as well as animals. In some areas ticks carry Lyme disease and Rocky Mountain spotted fever. It is important that you discuss the tick problem with your local veterinarian, who can advise you on which dangers might present themselves. New monthly topicals can almost eliminate the tick problem.

Vomiting and Diarrhea

Perhaps the most common canine ailments are vomiting and diarrhea. They do not indicate that your dog is seriously ill, but should either symptom persist for more than 24 hours, do not hesitate to call your veterinarian. Young puppies should be seen sooner as they can quickly dehydrate.

Evidence of blood, either "coffee ground" in appearance in vomit or black and tarlike in stools, warrants an immediate visit to your veterinarian.

Dogs may vomit to purge their digestive tracts. Puppies may do so when they eat too much or too fast. Intense exercise directly after eating can cause vomiting. None of this is cause for alarm unless it occurs repeatedly.

For occasional diarrhea, change from your dog's regular diet to thoroughly cooked rice with a small amount of boiled chicken added. Maintain this kind of diet until the condition improves and then gradually return your dog to its normal diet.

MEDICAL PROBLEMS

Minor accidents and illnesses will undoubtedly occur while your Australian Cattle Dog progresses through puppyhood, adolescence, and on into old age. This chapter is written in the hope that it will assist the owner of a pet Australian Cattle Dog to determine the difference between situations that can easily be taken care of at home and those that demand veterinary treatment.

There is one piece of advice that always applies: If you are in doubt about the seriousness of your dog's problem, do not hesitate to pick up the phone and call your veterinarian; he or she knows which questions to ask and will be able to determine whether or not it is necessary to see your dog.

Immunizations

Very effective vaccines have been developed to combat diseases that once were fatal to practically any infected dog. The danger of an Australian Cattle Dog being infected with distemper, hepatitis, leptospirosis, or the extremely virulent parvovirus is highly unlikely if proper inoculations and booster shots have been given regularly. Rabies among well-cared-for dogs is

Regular veterinary checkups will keep the Australian Cattle Dog happy and healthy.

practically unheard of, but dogs that come in contact with animals in nature can be at risk if not immunized. Your veterinarian may also recommend immunizations against kennel cough and coronavirus.

Immunization against these infectious diseases begins in puppyhood and it is extremely important that you follow your veterinarian's inoculation schedule; neglecting to do so could easily cost your dog's life. On occasion, however, there are dogs that, for one reason or another, do not develop full immunity. Any marked change in your dog's behavior should be observed very closely, especially if your dog is under a year of age.

Should your dog suddenly become listless, refuse food, and start to cough and sneeze, contact your veterinarian at once. Other signs of possible problems in this area are marked increase in thirst, blood in the stools or urine, and discharge of any kind from the nose.

Emergencies

Accidents

Injuries sustained in a road accident can be fatal if not handled correctly and promptly. If your dog is struck by an automobile or motorcycle, it is important that you remain calm. Panic on your part will serve only to upset the injured animal and could cause it to thrash around and injure itself even more seriously.

Often an injured animal is panicky and may snap at you. Muzzle the dog before lifting it to prevent any injury to yourself.

If your dog is unable to move itself, immediately remove it from the street where it could be further injured. In picking up your injured dog, it is critical that you support the body as fully as possible. The less movement of the injured area the better.

The Australian Cattle Dog is of a size that the average person can lift and support the dog without too much difficulty. If for some reason

When to Call Your Veterinarian
- ✔ Persistent coughing or sneezing
- ✔ Gasping for breath
- ✔ Vomiting
- ✔ Diarrhea
- ✔ Continued listlessness
- ✔ Loss of appetite
- ✔ Excessive thirst
- ✔ Runny nose
- ✔ Discharge from the eyes or ears
- ✔ Blood in the stool
- ✔ Limping, trembling, or shaking
- ✔ Abscesses, lumps, or swellings
- ✔ Dark or cloudy urine
- ✔ Difficult urination
- ✔ Loss of bowel or bladder control
- ✔ Deep red or white gums

you are alone and lifting your dog presents a problem, gently place it on a blanket and carefully slide the blanket to the vehicle that you will use to transport the dog to your veterinarian.

Do not wait to determine the extent of injury. Internal injuries may have occurred that you are unable to observe immediately. Get the injured dog to a veterinarian without delay. Ask someone to drive you there so that you are free to hold your injured dog and keep it calm. If there is no one else available to drive you, put the injured dog in a box or shipping kennel of some kind to keep it as immobile as possible.

Bleeding Wounds

If there is a bleeding wound due to a traffic accident or any other accident, deal with the

Never hesitate to take your Cattle Dog to a veterinarian in the case of an accident or if you suspect poisoning.

bleeding at once. Using a pad of cotton or a compress soaked in cold water, apply pressure directly to the bleeding point. If the flow of blood is not stemmed, your dog could bleed to death.

An Australian Cattle Dog seldom will pick fights with other dogs, but they are not inclined to back down when challenged. Should your dog be injured in a fight, get it to the veterinarian without delay. Bite wounds are invariably infected and antibiotic treatment is necessary.

Stings and Bites

Australian Cattle Dogs are curious animals and seem fascinated by all things that fly and crawl. They naturally attempt to examine insects with their paws or mouths. This can lead to bites and stings on the foot, or worse, on or around the mouth or nose.

If the stinger is visible, remove it with a pair of tweezers and apply a saline solution or mild antiseptic. If the swelling is large, particularly inside the mouth, or if the dog appears to be in shock, contact your veterinarian at once.

Foreign Objects

Should you see your Australian Cattle Dog pawing at its mouth or rubbing its mouth along the ground, immediately check to see if there is something lodged in the dog's mouth. Australian Cattle Dogs can shatter bones and objects that most other dogs would be incapable of doing and can manage to get the object lodged or trapped across their teeth, usually halfway back, or even at the back of the mouth where the two jaws hinge.

Should this be the case, grasp the object firmly between your fingers and push firmly toward the back of the mouth where the teeth

If Your Australian Cattle Dog Is Poisoned

Be prepared in the event that your Cattle Dog is poisoned:

1. Keep the telephone number of your local poison control center with your other emergency numbers.

2. If you know or suspect which poison your dog has ingested, give this information to the poison control center when you call them. They may be able to prescribe an immediate antidote.

3. Have the emergency number of your dog's veterinarian or the nearest 24-hour emergency veterinary hospital current and easily available. Give any information you receive from the poison control center to your veterinarian.

4. If you are not sure that your dog has been poisoned or which poison it may have ingested, describe the symptoms you are observing to your veterinarian.

5. Common symptoms of poisoning:
- Convulsions
- Paralysis
- Tremors
- Vomiting
- Diarrhea
- Stomach cramps and pains, accompanied by whimpering or howling, heavy breathing.

are wider. This will usually dislodge the object, but be sure to have a firm grip on the object so the dog does not swallow it. If you are unable to remove the object quickly, get the dog to the veterinarian at once.

If you suspect your dog has swallowed a small ball or some other object, check to see if the object is visible in the dog's throat. If so, reach in,

Any marked change in your dog's behavior should be observed very closely, especially if your dog is under one year of age.

grasp the object firmly, and pull it out. If the dog seems to be experiencing difficulty in breathing, the object may be lodged in the windpipe. Sharp blows to the rib cage may cause the dog to expel air from the lungs and also expel the object.

If any small object is missing in the home and you suspect your dog may have ingested it, do not hesitate to consult your veterinarian. An X-ray will reveal the hidden "treasure" and save your dog's life.

Illnesses

Rabies

It is important that you are aware of the clinical signs of rabies in animals and report any animal bites to your veterinarian. Generally speaking, there are two types of rabies: the violent type and what is referred to as the dumb type. In the violent type the afflicted animal goes wild, biting and attacking anything that moves. An animal with the dumb type of rabies will appear to be paralyzed and may sit staring without focus. The animal's lower jaw may hang open, emitting saliva.

Rabies shots are normally given when puppies are four to six months old. Again, the possibility of your Cattle Dog coming into contact with undomesticated animals may make earlier immunization a wise choice, and you should discuss this with your veterinarian.

Kennel Cough

Kennel cough (infectious rhinotracheitis), while highly infectious, is not a serious disease; it is like a mild case of influenza in humans. It is caused by a mixture of a bacteria and a virus. The name of the disease is misleading as it implies that a dog must be in a kennel environment to be infected. Actually, it is very easily passed from one dog to another in almost any situation.

The symptoms can make the disease sound far worse than it actually is. They are particularly nerve-wracking because there is a persistent hacking cough that at times makes one think that surely the dog will bring up everything it has ever eaten!

There are various protective procedures now available that can be administered by your veterinarian. In addition to inoculations, there is an intranasal vaccine available. These protective measures are advisable for your Australian Cattle Dog if you ever take it to a dog park or plan on placing it in a boarding kennel. Many boarding kennels now insist upon proof of protection against kennel cough before they will allow a dog to be admitted.

Coronavirus

Coronavirus, also referred to as coronaviral gastroenteritis, is a highly contagious virus and can be caused by ingesting fecal matter of an infected canid, which can also include coyotes and foxes. Dogs of any age can be infected and symptoms include watery stools, vomiting, and anorexia. Coronavirus can be successfully treated by a veterinarian but immunization is recommended to prevent the disease.

Internal Parasites

Tapeworms and heartworms are best diagnosed and treated by your veterinarian. Great advances are continually made in dealing with both of these parasites and what was once a complicated and time-consuming treatment has been simplified over the years. Most of the dog's internal

Life cycle of the tapeworm: fleas are commonly hosts of the tapeworm. When the flea is swallowed, the parasite is shared with your dog—tapeworms develop and segments are passed in the feces.

parasites are readily detected by your veterinarian's microscopic inspection of the dog's stool.

Tapeworms: Tapeworms are a part of the life cycle of the flea. If your dog has now or has had fleas in the past, it undoubtedly has tapeworms. A sign of infection is the appearance of segments of the worm crawling around the dog's anus or in the stool just after the dog has relieved itself. Your veterinarian can inoculate your Australian Cattle Dog if it has this problem, and the tapeworms are quickly and completely eliminated.

Whipworms: Whipworms are round and tapered in shape. These parasites normally settle in the cecum and upper part of the large intestine. They are extremely difficult to see other than by veterinary inspection of the stool. The parasites thrive on the host and can cause severe impairment of the dog's health and, in extreme cases, even death.

Roundworms: Roundworms are not an unusual condition in dogs and are rarely harmful in an adult dog; however, these parasites can cause extreme health hazards to puppies if present in large amounts.

Roundworms can be transmitted from mother to puppies so make sure that your female is free of roundworms before you breed her if you plan on a litter of puppies.

Hookworms: These tiny parasites attach themselves to the insides of the small intestines. They multiply rapidly and suck the blood of the infected dog. This can be extremely and quickly debilitating to puppies and young dogs. Stool sample examination by a veterinarian is recommended for any dog or puppy that continues to act listless.

Heartworms: Heartworms are parasitic worms found in dogs' hearts. The worm is transmitted by mosquitoes that carry the larvae of the worm.

Life cycle of the heartworm: infected mosquitoes bite your dog and deposit the heartworm larvae on its skin. The larvae enter the bloodstream through the hole created by the mosquito bite and make their way to the dog's heart.

Your veterinarian can detect the presence of heartworm by a blood test. There are preventive medications for a dog that tests negative for heartworms and corrective measures for the dog that has been infected.

Inherited Health Problems and Diseases

Like all breeds of domesticated dogs, the Australian Cattle Dog has its share of hereditary problems; fortunately, the problems are relatively few. Some fanciers are inclined to believe this is due to the proximity of the breed's dingo heritage. The dingo is free of incapacitating problems due to a process called natural selection. Any genetically transferred infirmity that would interfere with a wild dog's ability to nurse as a puppy, to capture food as an adult, or to escape from a predator, would automatically eliminate the individual from the gene pool.

We who control the breeding of our domesticated dogs are intent upon saving all the puppies in a litter, but in preserving life we also perpetuate health problems. Our humanitarian proclivities thus have a downside as well.

The diseases described here may not be present in the Australian Cattle Dog you buy, nor are these problems necessarily to be found in your Australian Cattle Dog's immediate ancestors. They are breed problems, however, that should be discussed with the breeder from whom you

It is amazing what some dogs will chew on and ingest. Consult your veterinarian for an X-ray if any small object is missing in the home and you suspect that your dog has swallowed it.

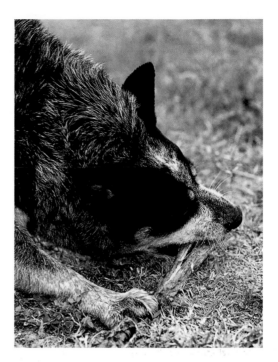

purchase your dog. As stated previously, the reputable Australian Cattle Dog breeder is aware of the following problems and should be more than willing to discuss them with you.

Deafness

The most serious congenital defect of the Australian Cattle Dog is deafness. This problem exists in collies, bull terriers, and Dalmatians, all three of which are known to have been used in the development of the Australian Cattle Dog.

It is extremely difficult to detect this problem when puppies are young, particularly while a puppy is still living with its littermates. An afflicted puppy is apt to respond in the same manner as it sees its littermates respond to a noise or situation.

Experienced breeders are aware that puppies can be tested for the problem even as early as five weeks old by using what is called the BAER (Brainstem Auditory Evoked Response) Test. Needless to say, a deaf dog makes a poor choice as a companion and afflicted animals should never be bred.

Hip Dysplasia

Hip dysplasia is a developmental disease of the hip joint. The result is instability of the hip joint due to abnormal contours of one or both of the hip joints. Some dogs might show tenderness in the hip, walk with a limp or swaying gait, or experience difficulty getting up. Symptoms vary from mild temporary lameness to severe crippling

in extreme cases. Treatment may require surgery. The problem is not rampant in the Australian Cattle Dog as a breed but enough cases have been reported to merit discussing it with any breeder you might consider buying a puppy from.

Progressive Retinal Atrophy

Progressive retinal atrophy, commonly referred to as "PRA," is a degenerative disease of the retinal cells of the eye that progresses to blindness. It usually occurs later in a Australian Cattle Dog's life—beyond the age of six years. Eye testing of breeding stock is now done by responsible breeders, which is a fortunate situation. Detecting the "carriers" of PRA and avoiding their use in a breeding program can all but eliminate the problem entirely. The new DNA tests will hopefully make PRA a rare disease in the near future.

SHARING YOUR LIFE WITH AN AUSTRALIAN CATTLE DOG

Everything in the Australian Cattle Dog's history and genetic makeup tells the same story—this is a working dog. If prospective dog owners are looking for a companion that loves to sit on its owner's lap all day or one that is content to lie patiently in front of the hearth while its owners are away, they should not consider an Australian Cattle Dog!

Enjoying the Breed's Versatility

The Australian Cattle Dog's heritage equips it to work all day in blistering sun or freezing winds. It innately knows what to do and how to do it. Do not expect an Australian Cattle Dog to harness that physical and psychic energy and keep it in reserve until its owner is ready for a restrained walk around the block.

There is no such thing as a Cattle Dog that has nothing to do. If a Cattle Dog's owner does

Australian Cattle Dogs are capable of sharing a wide range of activities with their owners.

not provide the dog with assigned duties, the dog will create its own activity schedule and, rest assured, more often than not the activities involved will seldom please the owner!

On the other hand, if the prospective owner of an Australian Cattle Dog is an active person who also derives as much pleasure from training a dog as this breed derives from being trained, this person will undoubtedly join the ranks of the thousands of Cattle Dog owners who consider the breed one of the most trainable and intelligent in existence.

Range of Activities

If an activity calls for speed, endurance, athletic ability, and intelligence, the Australian

The Australian Cattle Dog lives for the moment when his owner says, "OK, let's go!"

Cattle Dog is a great candidate. There is such a wide array of events an Australian Cattle Dog is capable of competing (and excelling) in that it is highly unlikely that even the owner whose energy and athletic ability registers at decathlon level will ever exhaust the Cattle Dog's potential.

What makes an Australian Cattle Dog such a versatile breed is its ability to perform well in a wide array of activities with complete ease. Your Cattle Dog can be a Canine Good Citizen certificate holder, conformation show competi-

tor, obedience trial star, speed demon on the agility course, herding trial whiz and Schutzhund candidate—and this is just scratching the surface of activities in which the Australian Cattle Dog can participate.

On a more serious note the Australian Cattle Dog's great scenting ability makes it a perfect candidate for drug and explosive detection as well as search-and-rescue work. Australian Cattle Dogs are also proving they can also make wonderful therapy dogs for the aged and infirmed.

Companions

The wonderful thing about all this is that the more involved and the more proficient your Australian Cattle Dog becomes in any or for that matter *all* of the above, the better it will become at being your best buddy and companion! While we have said time and time again that the Australian Cattle Dog is not a dog for everyone, we can also say the owner who is suited to this breed could not possibly hope to have a better dog.

It would be impossible to give all the detailed training instructions necessary to make your Australian Cattle Dog proficient in the many activities for which it is suitable. We will, however, endeavor to give a broad overview of the activities that many Cattle Dogs have excelled in and leave it up to the owners to pursue any of them in which they have an interest. Additional information on these activities can be found in Information, beginning on page 92.

Conformation Shows

Popular and well-attended dog events are the combined conformation shows and obedience trials that are regulated by the American Kennel Club (AKC) and the United Kennel Club (UKC).

The original purpose of conformation shows was to give breeders a means of comparing their stock to that of other fanciers and thereby make improvements in their breeding programs.

Today, not all people who participate in conformation shows intend to become breeders. Many simply find enjoyment in the competitive aspect of these events. Referred to by some as "canine beauty contests," conformation dog shows take place nearly every weekend of the year in one part of the country or another and are open to all non-neutered, AKC- and UKC-registered dogs.

Generally speaking, conformation shows fall into two major categories: matches and championship events. Match shows are primarily staged for the young or inexperienced dogs that are not ready to compete for championship points. In most cases, classes are offered for dogs from about three months of age and older.

Match Shows

Matches are an excellent place for novice handlers to learn to show their own dogs. Since these match shows are far more informal than championship events, there is plenty of time for the novice handler to ask questions and seek assistance from more experienced exhibitors or from the officiating judges.

Match shows can be held for all breeds or they can be what are referred to as "specialty matches," which are for one particular breed of dog. When there is a club devoted to a specific breed in an area, that club will often hold these match shows so that the newer club members and the young puppies will have an opportunity to gain some experience.

Information regarding these matches can usually be found in the classified sections of Sunday newspapers under "Dogs for Sale." Local breeders are usually aware of upcoming events of this kind as well.

There is no need to enter these informal matches ahead of time. Most accept entries on the grounds of the show site the morning of the event. The person taking your entry will be able to assist you in filling out the entry form and give you the preliminary instructions you will need.

Championship Shows

Championship shows are much more formal in nature and best entered after you have gained some experience by participating in several match events. Championship shows are sponsored by various all-breed kennel clubs or in some instances by a club specializing in one particular breed of dog. The AKC and the UKC can provide you with the name of the all-breed kennel club in your area and the Australian Cattle Dog Club of America can let you know if there is an Australian Cattle Dog specialty club in your vicinity (see Information, page 92).

How a Champion Is Made

A registered dog can become a champion of record by winning a given number of championship "points." These points are awarded to the best male and best female nonchampions in each breed. The number of championship points that can be won at a particular show is based upon the number of entries in a dog's own breed and sex entered at the show and the area in which the show is located. These requirements are determined by the organization sponsoring the event, primarily the AKC or UKC.

Catalogs sold at all championship shows list the particulars relevant to every dog entered in the show. The catalog also lists the number of dogs required in each breed to win from one through five points. Since the number of dogs necessary for the various number of points differs geographically, it is important to check the catalog at each show you attend at which your male or female has been awarded points.

Canine Good Citizen Test

Though this event does not achieve any official title, it is nonetheless an extremely valuable accomplishment. The purpose of the test is to demonstrate that the canine entered is well mannered and an asset to the community. There are ten parts to the test and the dog must pass all ten in order to be awarded a certificate:

1. Appearance and grooming
2. Acceptance of a stranger
3. Walking on a loose leash; heel and execute turns and halts.
4. Walking through a crowd
5. Sitting for examination
6. Sitting and lying down on command
7. Staying in both the *sit* and *down* position
8. Positive reaction to another dog
9. Calm reaction to distracting sights or noises
10. Ability to be left alone (tied with leash while owner is out of sight)

Trials and Events

Obedience

Obedience trials are held at both championship shows and matches, as are the conformation events. The same informal entry procedures that apply to conformation matches apply here as well. The championship or "sanctioned" obedience trials are normally held in conjunction with conformation events and normally require pre-entry.

Obedience training classes are definitely prerequisites here, since competition is highly precise and based entirely upon your dog's performing a set series of exercises. The exercises required in the various classes of competition range from basics like *heel*, *sit*, and *lie down* in the novice class on through the sophisticated exercises of the utility and tracking dog levels that require scent discrimination and directed jumping.

Each level has a degree that can be earned after attaining qualifying scores at a given number of shows. The competition levels and corresponding degrees are: Novice earning a Companion Dog degree (CD), Open that earns the Companion Dog Excellent degree (CDX), and Utility earning the Utility Dog and Utility Dog Excellent degrees (UD and UDX). Tracking events earn the rare Tracking Dog and Tracking Dog Excellent titles (TD and TDX).

Agility

Agility competition is actually an obstacle course for dogs. Everyone involved (and everyone who watches) appears to be having the time of their lives. There are 14 obstacles that the canine contestants must master off-leash while being timed. The course includes tunnels, cat walks, seesaws, hoops, and numerous other obstacles. Still in the early stages of growth, this event is catching on rapidly and will undoubtedly become one of the biggest attractions at all breed dog shows.

Herding Tests and Trials

It goes without saying that herding trials employ the very essence of the Australian Cattle Dog. Australian Cattle Dog breeders encourage

Australian Cattle Dogs excel in Herding Tests and Trials.

every owner of the breed to participate in these events as the trials preserve and perpetuate the breed's celebrated herding instincts.

Herding trials are sponsored by the AKC and are open to dogs over nine months of age that are registered with the organization as a herding breed. There are three levels of competition involved in the AKC's program: Herding Tested, Pre-trial Testing, and Herding Trials.

Herding test: This test is quite simple as it is designed to reveal the dog's willingness to respond to its handler and its ability to control the movement of the livestock involved—cattle, goats, sheep, or even ducks.

In order to pass the test the dog must successfully accomplish the following:

1. Execute a *stay* on command.
2. Follow two commands to change the direction of the moving stock.
3. Stop on command.
4. Come on recall.

Ten minutes are allowed for the exercises. The dog must successfully pass two such tests under two different judges and no score is given; the test is either passed or failed. After passing both tests, the participating dog is awarded the Herding Tested (HT) degree, which becomes an official title and can be added to its registered name.

Pre-trial test: In this event the dog must:

1. Work the livestock through obstacles.
2. Stop the stock.
3. Turn the stock.
4. Reverse the direction of the stock.
5. Pen the stock within ten minutes.

This is also a pass or fail event that must be successfully completed under two different judges and earns the official Pre-trial Tested (PT) title.

Herding trial: Dogs competing in the Herding Trial events have three options in which to compete designated as the A, B, or C courses. The three courses are designed to show different areas of working ability.

Each of the courses has three levels of accomplishment: Herding Started (HS), Herding Intermediate (HI), and Advanced. Proficiency in the Advanced level earns the dog a Herding Excellent (HX).

The Australian Cattle Dog loves games that include retrieving. Playing Frisbee can keep a Cattle Dog interested for hours.

All of these trials must be completed with a score of at least 60 out of a possible 100 points, which are divided into six categories of proficiency. A dog must earn at least half of the points allotted to each of the six categories in order to qualify.

The courses involve complex patterns, many of which require a participating dog to respond to verbal commands from the handler while keeping his eye on the stock. Details of these complex trials can be obtained from the AKC's Herding Department and there are numerous books and periodicals on the subject listed in the last chapter of this book. The AKC also sponsors herding trial clinics at various locations throughout the United States through the year.

Schutzhund

The purpose of Schutzhund training is to test a dog's ability in the area of obedience, tracking, and protection. There are three levels of proficiency (Schutzhund I, II, and III) in each of the

three parts and a dog is tested in all three parts at the same trial. A passing score is required in each of the three parts in order to acquire the Schutzhund degree.

It is very important to understand that the purpose of Schutzhund training is to develop a well-adjusted and well-trained dog friendly to all who have no hostile intentions. A Schutzhund dog is *not* an attack dog; it performs on command—and only on command—and is not a loose cannon exploding at will. Schutzhund training is not to be taken lightly nor undertaken without qualified supervision.

Fun and Games

Your Australian Cattle Dog will play games far longer than you may want to, but it is certainly a way in which you can both stay fit and you can help release some of your dog's stored-up energy.

Frisbee: An Australian Cattle Dog will retrieve a Frisbee for hours on end and the breed is especially adept at learning how to catch the thrown Frisbee. There are competitions and even national championships offered for dogs excelling in the sport.

However, a word of caution concerning Frisbees: Playing Frisbee and other sports that require jumping should not be played for more than very brief periods, at most, with young puppies. Knee injuries are not uncommon among Australian Cattle Dogs, especially dogs who do not have properly angulated hindquarters.

Flyball: Flyball is a race in which two teams of four dogs race over hurdles to trigger a box that releases a ball that they carry back over the hurdles. The Australian Cattle Dog is a star at this event.

Hiking: The dedicated outdoors man or woman could not possibly have a better companion than the Australian Cattle Dog. The breed will enjoy hiking as much as any human and its human companion does not have the worry of the Cattle Dog wandering off and disappearing for hours on end; the Cattle Dog wants to be with its owner—*always*.

Swimming: If the Australian Cattle Dog owner enjoys a day at the beach or in the surf, the Australian Cattle Dog will also be right there. The breed loves water and is an excellent swimmer. Owners who live near a lake or pond find that their Cattle Dogs will usually take several swimming breaks a day when temperatures rise.

While we caution prospective dog owners that the Australian Cattle Dog is not a breed for everyone, those who are suited to the breed are to be envied. They couldn't have a better canine friend and companion.

Non-Competitive Pursuits

Therapy and Assistance Dogs

There are other, non-athletic pursuits that some Australian Cattle Dog owners have found to be meaningful ways to share time with their dogs. The fields of Therapy and Assistance are just two ways that owner and dog can work together for the good of mankind.

Therapy dogs are trained to visit the sick, those with disabilities, and the aged. Many Cattle Dogs have proven that they adapt themselves to this role with ease. It depends, of course, upon the individual dog—some love making these visits, while others are better suited to the more active competitive pursuits.

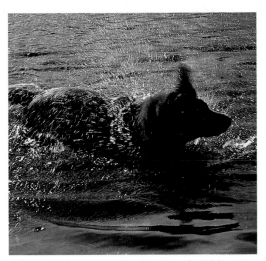

Always use caution in selecting the places you allow your Cattle Dog to swim. Currents and riptides can overpower even the best of swimmers.

Therapy Dogs International registers dogs that are temperamentally suitable for visiting hospitals and nursing homes. It has been found that there is great therapeutic value to the patients who come in contact with these dogs. Medical journals have substantiated stress reduction and lowered blood pressure as a result of these human-to-animal associations. Information regarding Therapy Dogs International can be found at the back of this book.

Australian Cattle Dogs can be trained in a wide range of assistance roles. Their keen vision and hearing make them ideal companions for the hard-of-hearing and the sight impaired, warning their owners of situations or sounds that they might otherwise not be capable of recognizing.

Kennel Clubs and Organizations

American Herding Breed Association
Siouxsan Eisen
E-mail: siouxsan@ahba-herding.org

American Kennel Club
51 Madison Avenue
New York, NY 10010
(212) 696-8200
www.akc.org

All registration information:
5580 Centerview Drive
Raleigh, NC 27606
(919) 233-9767

Australian Cattle Dog Club of America Rescue League
ivy@acdrescueinc.com - Bay Area, California
stacey@acdrescueinc.com - Mid-Florida
brooke@acdrescueinc.com - Seattle,
 Washington
mary@acdrescueinc.com - Raleigh, North
 Carolina
joann@acdrescueinc.com - St. Louis, Missouri
www.acdrescueinc.com

Australian National Kennel Council
 The Australian National Kennel Council is the administrative body for pure breed canine affairs in Australia. It does not, however, deal directly with dog exhibitors, breeders, or judges. For information pertaining to breeders, clubs, or shows, please contact the relevant State or Territory Controlling Body.

AUSTRALIAN CAPITAL TERRITORY
ACT Canine Association Inc
P.O. Box 815
Dickson ACT 2602
www.actca.asn.au

NEW SOUTH WALES
Dogs NSW
P.O. Box 632
St. Marys NSW 1790
www.dogsnsw.org.au

NORTHERN TERRITORY
The North Australian Canine Association, Inc.
P.O. Box 37521
Winnellie NT 0821
www.users.bigpond.com/naca1/

QUEENSLAND
Canine Control Council (Queensland)
P.O. Box 495
Fortitude Valley Qld 4006
www.cccq.org.au

SOUTH AUSTRALIA
South Australian Canine Association Inc
P.O. Box 844
Prospect East SA 5082
www.saca.caninenet.com

TASMANIA
Tasmanian Canine Association, Inc.
The Rothman Building
P.O. Box 116
Glenorchy Tas 7010
www.tascanineassoc.org

VICTORIA
Victorian Canine Association
Locked Bag K9
Cranbourne VIC 3977
www.vca.org.au

WESTERN AUSTRALIA
Canine Association of Western Australia
    (Inc)
P.O. Box 1404
Canning Vale WA 6970
www.cawa.asn.au

Canadian Kennel Club
89 Skyway Avenue, Unit 100
Etobicoke, Ontario
Canada M9W 6R4
(416) 675-5511

The Kennel Club
1-5 Clargis Street
Piccadilly, London W1Y 8AB
England

New Zealand Kennel Club
Prosser Street, Private Bag 50903
Porirua 6220
www.nzkc@nzkc.org.nz

United Kennel Club
100 E. Kilgore Road
Kalamazoo, MI 49001-5598
(269) 343-9020
www.ukcdogs.com

United Schutzhund Clubs of America
c/o Paul Meloy
3704 Lemay Ferry Road
St. Louis, MO 63125

United States Dog Agility Association
c/o Heather Smith
Public Relations & Communications
(972) 487-2200 Ext. #10
www.usdaa.com

INDEX

Accidents, 78
Activity, 49
Adult dog, 27, 32–33, 56–57
Aggression, 50, 54
Agility competition, 88
Alone, 51–52, 56
Altering, 24, 53
Anal sacs, 71
Assistance dogs, 91

Bathing, 70
Behavior problems, 50–52
Bites, 79
Bleeding wounds, 78–79
Boundary setting, 50
Breeders, 25, 31
Brushing, 68
Buying
  adult dog, 32–33
  considerations before, 20–21, 23–24
  male vs. female, 24
  show dog vs. companion, 28–31
  sources for, 24–25

Cage, 37–38, 52
Canine Good Citizen, 88
Car travel, 41–42
Championship shows, 87
Chasing, 41
Chewing, 40, 50–51
Children, 33, 46–47
Coat, 17, 38
Collar, 38, 65
Colors, 17
Commands
  Come, 34–35
  Down, 65
  Heel, 65
  Sit, 63–64
  Stay, 64
Conformation shows, 86–87
Coronavirus, 81
Crate, 43–45

Dalmatian, 10–11
Deafness, 28, 83
Dental care, 71–72
Diarrhea, 75
Diet
  for older dog, 57
  specialty, 61
Digging, 52
Dingo, 6–8

Ear(s)
  cleaning of, 71
  inspection of, 28
Ear mites, 75
Emergencies, 78–80
Equipment
  for grooming, 67–68
  for puppy, 37–38
Estrus cycles, 53
Exercise, 56–57
Eyes, 15, 71

Feeding, 43
Fipronil, 74
Fleas, 72–74
Food
  amount of, 59–60
  canned, 60–61
  dry, 60–61
  nutrients, 60
Foot care, 68–69
Foreign objects, 79–80

Gait, 17
Games, 90–91
Grooming, 38, 67–70
Grooming table, 67–68

Head, 15
Health certificates, 31–32
Health check, 31
Health problems, 57
Heartworms, 82
Herding tests and trials, 88–90
Hip dysplasia, 83
History, 5–6, 8–11, 13
Home health care, 71–72

Hookworms, 82
Housebreaking, 42–45, 51

Illnesses, 80–82
Imidacloprid, 74
Immunizations, 77
Inherited conditions, 82–83
Inoculations, 31–32

Jumping up, 51

Kennel, 37–38, 43, 52
Kennel cough, 80–81

Leadership, 23–24
Leash, 38, 49, 65
Leash training, 35
Lice, 75
Lufenuron, 73

Males, 24
Match shows, 87

Nail trimming, 68–69
Neutering, 24, 53

Obedience training, 33–35, 50, 54–55
Obedience trials, 88
Outdoor activity, 49–50
Overweight dog, 61

Parasites, 72–75, 81–82
Pedigree, 32
Pets, 40–41
Poisoning, 79
Price, 31
Progressive retinal atrophy, 83
Protein, 60
Puppy
  age of, 28–29
  diet sheet for, 32, 38
  housebreaking, 42–45, 51
  inoculations, 31–32
  male vs. female, 24
  pedigree for, 32
  preparations for, 37–38

purebred, 21–23
registration certificate, 32
show dog vs. companion, 28–31
socialization of, 46–47
training of, 34–35
transporting of, 39
"Puppy-Proofing," 39–40
Purebred dog, 21–23
Pyometra, 57

Rabies, 80
Red speckle, 17
Registration certificate, 32
Roundworms, 82

Schutzhund, 90
Shipping kennel, 37–38
Show dog, 28–31
Size, 17
Socialization, 46–47
Spaying, 24, 53
Stings, 79
Strangers, 47

Tail, 16
Tapeworms, 81
Teeth, 71–72
Temperament, 15
Territoriality, 27
Therapy dogs, 91
Ticks, 75
Toys, 38, 53
Training, 33–35, 54–55
Training collar, 65
Transporting, 39, 42
Traveling, 41–42, 55–56

Vaccinations, 29
Versatility, 14, 85–86
Veterinary health check, 31
Vomiting, 75

Water dish, 38
Whipworms, 81
Wounds, 78–79

About the Author

Richard G. Beauchamp has been a lifelong dog breeder and exhibitor. He has judged all breeds of purebred dogs in every major country of the world and written about dogs and dog breeding for publications in many countries, including Australia, England, and the United States. He has observed the Australian Cattle Dog at work on the huge ranches in the breed's homeland and has also visited organizations in Australia that have been officially entrusted with the protection of the dingo as a native animal.

Acknowledgments

The author wishes to acknowledge the assistance of Norman and Carolyn Herbel and Marge Blankenship for their assistance in making this project a reality. Their knowledge of the breed and dedication to maintaining the true character and working ability of the Australian Cattle Dog provided the inspiration and basis for my research. I also wish to thank my editor Annemarie McNamara for her assistance and patience in completing this project.

Photo Credits

Norvia Behling: 2–3, 12, 20, 26, 36, 40, 43, 45, 59, 80, 83, and 86; Kent Dannen: 4, 8, 16, 21, 23, 25, 33, 41, 52, 63, 72, 78, 89, and 91; Tara Darling: 17 and 57; Cheryl Ertelt: 29, 73, 84, and 93; Isabelle Francais: 13, 19, 22, 27, 30, 51, and 76; Karen Hudson: 7; Pets by Paulette: 5, 6, 15, 18, 37, 39, 44, 48, 49, 58, 62, 66, 67, 69, 70 (top and bottom), 71, 74, 77, and 85.

Cover Photos

Front cover and back cover: Tara Darling; inside front cover: Karen Hudson; inside back cover: Norvia Behling.

© Copyright 2007, 1997 by Barron's Educational Series, Inc.

All rights reserved.
No part of this book may be reproduced in any form, by photostat, microfilm, xerography, or any other means, or incorporated into any information retrieval system, electronic or mechanical, without the written permission of the copyright owner.

All inquiries should be addressed to:
Barron's Educational Series, Inc.
250 Wireless Boulevard
Hauppauge, NY 11788
www.barronseduc.com

ISBN-13: 978-0-7641-3649-8
ISBN-10: 0-7641-3649-6

Library of Congress Catalog Card No. 2007014543

Library of Congress Cataloging-in-Publication Data
Beauchamp, Richard G.
    Australian Cattle Dogs : everything about purchase, care, nutrition, behavior, and training / Richard G. Beauchamp ; illustrations by Michele Earle-Bridges.
        p. cm.
    Includes bibliographical references and index.
    ISBN-13: 978-0-7641-3649-8 (alk. paper)
    ISBN-10: 0-7641-3649-6 (alk. paper)
    1. Australian Cattle Dog. I. Title.

SF429.A77B43 2007
636.737—dc22   2007014543

Printed in China
9 8 7 6 5 4 3 2